On Earth as it is in Heaven

Jubilee Edition

JOSEPHINE LOMBARDI

PAULIST PRESS
New York / Mahwah, NJ

To Margaret O'Gara,
in loving memory

© 2023 Novalis Publishing Inc.

Cover design and layout: Audrey Wells
Cover image: iStock/Aleksandar Georgiev

Published by Novalis

Publishing Office
1 Eglinton Avenue East, Suite 800
Toronto, Ontario, Canada
M4P 3A1

Head Office
4475 Frontenac Street
Montréal, Québec, Canada
H2H 2S2

en.novalis.ca

Library of Congress Control Number: 2023941274

ISBN 987-0-8091-5669-6 (paperback)
ISBN 978-0-8091-8830-7 (e-book)

Published in the United States by
Paulist Press
997 Macarthur Boulevard
Mahwah, New Jersey 07430

www.paulistpress.com

Printed in Canada.

Contents

Foreword

Pope Francis wanted the year immediately preceding the Jubilee of 2025 to be dedicated to a "great 'symphony' of prayer," thus showing the most authentic nature of the Jubilee event. In fact, it is a "special gift of grace" with which God supports and encourages the journey of all people, who in recent years have experienced profound turmoil and bewilderment, also due to the COVID-19 pandemic. And if it is certain that God offers his love and grace without measure, the People of God need instead to prepare themselves to welcome these gifts, opening wide the doors of their hearts to the Redeemer.

This is the reason why, in churches all over the world, courses and aids are prepared to help people rediscover prayer as the "royal road to holiness" and as an introduction to the Jubilee event. This volume, *On Earth as it is in Heaven*, which Josephine Lombardi presents in an updated version, has already helped many people in the recent past to rediscover the value of prayer. Now it is reproposed as a Jubilee Edition, accepting Pope Francis' invitation to "make the 'Our Father', the prayer Jesus taught us, the life programme of each of his disciples."

I like to think of the Our Father as the prayer of pilgrims who mark the steps of their journey, sanctifying the Lord's name, building his Kingdom, and trying to fulfill his will. When it comes to the rhythm of this filial prayer, I think of when pilgrims reach St. Peter's Basilica to go through the Holy Door, experiencing God's mercy and his forgiveness. I see them go to the Tombs of the Apostles to profess the faith of the Church together, placing the seal of the 'Amen' on the entire journey they have travelled.

The Catechism of the Catholic Church teaches that precisely "from this unshakeable faith springs forth the hope that sustains each of the seven petitions" of the Our Father (CCC 2772). While, on the one hand, these petitions "express the groanings of the present age, this time of patience and expectation," on the other hand, they attest to the certainty of the salvation that God has already achieved in Christ. This is the deepest meaning of Christian hope, which is not the virtue of those who delude themselves but of those who, in the depths of their hearts, are certain that God is faithful.

We are grateful to Josephine Lombardi, who accompanies the reader by commenting on the individual petitions of the Lord's Prayer, helping the reader to discover their innermost meanings. In this way, the commentary allows the prayer to delicately enter the folds of the human soul and its wounds. I am sure that meditating on these pages will allow us to deepen the meaning of the Our Father for Christian life, helping to "fan the flame of hope," as Pope Francis has exhorted the Church to do on the occasion of the Jubilee of 2025.

Archbishop Salvatore Rino Fisichella
Pro-Prefect of the Dicastery for Evangelization
May 2023

Preface to
the Jubilee Edition

On February 11, 2022, Pope Francis announced preparations for an upcoming Jubilee Year to be celebrated in 2025, with the motto "Pilgrims of Hope." In his letter to Archbishop Salvatore Rino Fisichella, Pro-Prefect for the Dicastery for Evangelization, for the Jubilee of 2025, he requested a preparatory year to take place in 2024, focusing on the need for prayer, especially reflection on the Lord's Prayer:

> As is customary, the Bull of Indiction, to be issued in due course, will contain the necessary guidelines for celebrating the Jubilee of 2025. In this time of preparation, I would greatly desire that we devote 2024, the year preceding the Jubilee event, to a great "symphony" of prayer. Prayer, above all else, to renew our desire to be in the presence of the Lord, to listen to him and to adore him. Prayer, moreover, to thank God for the many gifts of his love for us and to praise his work in creation, which summons everyone to respect it and to take concrete and responsible steps to protect it. Prayer as the expression of a single "heart and soul" (cf. *Acts* 4:32), which then translates into solidarity and the sharing of our daily bread. Prayer that makes it possible for every man and woman in this world to turn to the one God and to reveal to him what lies hidden in the depths of their heart. Prayer as the royal road to holiness, which enables us to be contemplative even in the midst of activity. *In a word, may it be an intense year of prayer in which hearts are opened to receive*

> *the outpouring of God's grace and to make the "Our Father," the prayer Jesus taught us, the life programme of each of his disciples.*[1]

When my dear friend Dr. Anne Jamieson, the executive director of the Institute for Catholic Education in Ontario, heard this news, she called me and said, "Why don't you prepare a special, updated jubilee edition of *On Earth as it is in Heaven*?" I forwarded this proposal to Joseph Sinasac, publishing director of Novalis Publishing, and he agreed.

What follows is a revised and updated version of the 2010 edition. While I am touched by the comments from the many readers who enjoyed the first edition, I am especially grateful for the opportunity to revisit it, tweaking, rewriting, reworking, and inserting new and fresh context, insights, and stories.

The first edition was inspired by another proposal—that of my doctoral thesis supervisor, Dr. Margaret O'Gara (1947–2012)—who encouraged me to develop an insight I shared in the concluding chapter of my doctoral dissertation: that salvation is the fulfillment of the Lord's Prayer in individuals, communities, and all of God's creation, in this lifetime and the next. Her proposal was further confirmed and buoyed by the date selected for my defense—October 5, 2005. On that day, Luke's account of the Lord's Prayer was the gospel reading. Feeling anxious about the outcome of my defense, I decided to attend Mass beforehand and was touched and inspired by the gospel reading, which caused me to ponder Margaret's proposal with greater enthusiasm. Moreover, it was the feast day of St. Faustina Kawalska, a messenger of God's endless mercy, another key insight shared in my dissertation on the topic of the universal salvific will of God. After my defense, Margaret continued to support me, and she was delighted to see the insight develop into a deeper reflection on the Lord's Prayer, helping the reader to grow in our understanding of God's gift of salvation, of which Jesus is the source.

This Jubilee edition, while keeping some of the content and stories of the first edition, offers a fuller reflection on the two halves of the prayer—how to honour and glorify God, including following God's will, and how to ask for what we need to be nourished, healed, forgiven, and delivered. Consequently, the lengthy commentary on salvation that is found in the first edition has been dispersed, with insights inserted throughout the book, including the concluding chapter. This allowed me more space to offer more context and details and to develop certain insights and Church teaching that were originally presented in a more simplified manner in the first edition.

My hope is that this book will be a resource for those seeking to deepen their understanding of the profound relevance and spiritual insight of the Lord's Prayer, helping them to see the logic and flow of the petitions and how one petition builds on the previous one, setting us up to experience fulfillment and authentic freedom. No doubt there will be other resources and riches of our tradition shared throughout the preparatory year and beyond. Nevertheless, I offer this reflection on the Lord's Prayer as a contribution to this very important time of preparation. Let's begin our study of the "life programme" that is revealed in this very important prayer.

Introduction to the Lord's Prayer

If we recite the Our Father but once within the space of an hour, it is sufficient, provided on the one hand that we understand that we are with him, and know what we are asking of him; and on the other, that he be desirous of granting it, and that he derives great pleasure from our company. He does not like to have us rack our brains in addressing long discourses to him.[1]

St. Augustine wrote, "Run through all the words of the holy prayers [in scripture], and I do not think that you will find anything in them that is not contained and included in the Lord's Prayer."[2] Similarly, St. Thomas Aquinas spoke of his own reverence for this prayer:

The Lord's Prayer is the most perfect of prayers … In it we ask, not only for all the things we can rightly desire, but also in the sequence that they should be desired. This prayer not only teaches us to ask for things, but also in what order we should ask them.[3]

In other words, he is saying, "the order in which the petitions appear is not arbitrary."[4] The Lord's Prayer, also known as the Our Father, is a prayer about relationships: namely, a correct relationship with God, including a participation in God's being—foundational for the flourishing of all relationships. Moreover, it is also about a correct relationship with our neighbours and a sharing in God's blessings. Our relationships on earth are to mirror the communion or fellowship experienced in heaven. Accordingly, the fulfillment of the petitions of the Lord's Prayer is to bring about a foretaste of heaven.

Origins of the Lord's Prayer

There are two versions of the Lord's Prayer, as found in Luke 11:2-4 and Matthew 6:9-13, each with its own unique context. Both compiled somewhere between 75 and 85 AD, the shorter version, found in Luke, comes in response to a disciple who asks Jesus, "Lord, teach us to pray, as John taught his disciples," (Luke 11:1). In this account Jesus responds:

> "Father, hallowed be your name.
> Your kingdom come.
> Give us each day our daily bread.
> And forgive us our sins, for we ourselves forgive everyone indebted to us.
> And do not bring us to the time of trial." (Luke 11:2-4)

It appears that this shorter version is intended for those who do not know how to pray, possibly the Gentile or non-Jewish audience of Luke's gospel, who need some simple formula to help them develop their prayer life.

The longer version, found in Matthew, is situated within Jesus' Sermon on the Mount, his teachings found in chapters 5, 6, and 7. The Sermon on the Mount is divided into four teaching blocks: how to be; how to love; how to pray; how to live. Addressed to people who pray but need more direction and clarity, this version of the prayer, not surprisingly, is found in the "how to pray" section:

> "Pray then in this way:
> Our Father in heaven,
> hallowed be your name.
> Your will be done, on earth as it is in heaven.
> Give us this day our daily bread.
> And forgive us our debts, as we also have forgiven our debtors.
> And do not bring us to the time of trial, but rescue us from the evil one."

Although translations of the original Greek may vary,[5] the Catholic Church uses the translation of the Latin text of the Roman Missal, the version that Catholic Christians use most often in public and private prayer. The prayer resembles more closely the versions found in the Douay-Rheims Bible and the King James Version of the Bible:

Our Father, who art in heaven,
hallowed be thy name;
thy kingdom come,
thy will be done
on earth as it is in heaven.
Give us this day our daily bread,
and forgive us our trespasses,
as we forgive those who trespass against us;
and lead us not into temptation,
but deliver us from evil.

Early Use of the Lord's Prayer

The Lord's Prayer, as "the summary of the whole Gospel,"[6] is a foundational prayer for Christians, as evidenced in the first-century noncanonical document the *Didache*, or *The Teaching of the Twelve Apostles*. According to the document, the prayer was included in the liturgical life of early Christians and has remained in the Church's liturgical prayer ever since. The *Didache*, dated between 50 and 100 AD, depending on your source,[7] documents how the first Christian communities began to pray the Lord's Prayer three times a day in place of a Jewish prayer with eighteen blessings,[8] known as the *Shemoneh Esre*, a prayer recited by Jews in Jesus' time. Its basic structure is divided into three general types: praise, petitions, and thanksgiving. Encouraging Jews to focus on repentance, forgiveness, and healing, the prayers affirm the holiness of God's name, culminating in a final blessing expressing thanksgiving for peace. Not surprisingly, the Lord's Prayer follows a similar pattern.

Early Christians memorized the Lord's Prayer, which helped them to reflect on the gospel as Jesus' main teaching points were summarized within the petitions of the prayer. Rich in spiritual insight, in the early Church, "the Lord's Prayer was taught to the catechumens at the conclusion of the catechumenate, in a ceremony that took place one week before the Easter vigil."[9] In some cases, it is reported that the Lord's Prayer was the first prayer recited after baptism.[10] Thankfully, the prayer remains a treasured pillar for Christians, deserving of more reflection and study.

Reflecting on the Petitions of the Lord's Prayer

What follows is a mostly non-technical and hopefully accessible reflection on the petitions of the Lord's Prayer. Resembling the arrangement of the decalogue or the Ten Commandments, the seven petitions of the Lord's Prayer are presented in two halves, each strategically positioned to build on the previous one. The first three petitions centre on God and God's kingdom, showing us how to have a correct relationship with God. The second half, consisting of the remaining four petitions, shows us how to have a correct relationship with our neighbour, concluding with a prayer of protection or deliverance against evil. Nevertheless, let us begin by acknowledging our Creator.

Our Father in Heaven

But when the fullness of time had come, God sent his Son, born of a woman, born under the law, in order to redeem those who were under the law, so that we might receive adoption as children. And because you are children, God has sent the Spirit of his Son into our hearts, crying, *"Abba! Father!"* So you are no longer a slave but a child, and if a child then also an heir, through God. (Galatians 4:4-7)

Abba is Aramaic, the language of Galilean peasants—Jesus' language—for "Father." St. Paul uses the same language, "Abba! Father!" in Romans 8:15, and in Mark's gospel, Jesus prays, "Abba, Father, for you all things are possible; remove this cup from me; yet, not what I want, but what you want" (14:36). Jesus addresses God as Father in each of his seventeen prayers.[11] Evidently, this was his preferred address for God. While, in the past, some scholars translated *Abba* as "daddy," noting how this was and is the familiar address used by some Mediterranean children when referencing their fathers,[12] other scholars translate *Abba* as "dear Father" or "dearest Father," resisting the inclination to translate the address as "daddy."[13] While some people find the address "daddy" endearing and intimate, indicating a deeper connection with God, others insist that it lacks reverence for God.[14] Murray Harris, for example, suggests that the biblical writers would have used the Greek *pappas* if "daddy" was intended.[15] Nevertheless, the Greek found in Matthew's account of the Lord's Prayer is *pater hēmōn* (6:9). This could be translated as "our dear Father."

Regardless of preference, we are reminded that Jesus called us to be like children: "Truly I tell you, unless you change and become like children, you will never enter the kingdom of heaven. Whoever becomes humble like this child is the greatest in the kingdom of heaven" (Matthew 18:3-4). The address *Abba* translated as "dear Father" is a more reverential presentation, inspiring awe and wonder, while "daddy," the term used by Mediterranean children addressing their fathers, challenges us to embrace a more intimate relationship with God. After all, scholars remind us that *Abba* belongs to the language of childhood.[16] What some may interpret as reverential, however, others may interpret as communicating distance. How many of us today call our parents "Mother" or "Father"? In Italian, father is *padre* and mother is *madre*. As a child, I addressed my parents as *papà* and *mamma* or *mammina* (Daddy and Mom/Mommy in Italian). It would have felt so formal and strange to address them as *madre* or *padre*. Moreover, as a mother of four adult children, I love being called "Mum." It signals connection and trust, knowing I am approachable and loving. Perhaps it is for this reason that Isaiah used feminine imagery to capture God's love for us: "As a mother comforts her child, so I will comfort you" (Isaiah 66:13).

Whether it is during times of difficulty, times of rejoicing, or moments of reminiscing, we often desire parental comfort, even after our parents are long gone. Just the other day, I smiled as I witnessed my 85-year-old mother-in-law sharing old photos of her deceased mother with family, referring to her mother as "my mommy" in Italian. We use language to communicate closeness and intimacy. Knowing how language can be used to deepen our understanding of God's being helps us to not lose sight of the key message: the desired end here is not only reverence for God but also closeness and intimacy with God. This begins with a correct understanding of God, which includes an image that is rooted in truth and is inspired by love.

Pondering God as our loving Father helps to heal our image of God, especially if it is false. Some may have been conditioned to perceive God as full of wrath and vengeance, distant and ready to punish and condemn. Catechesis is required to correct false images, reminding the faithful that God is not only just but also merciful, waiting for us to approach like a trusting child. Proper catechesis helps us to reflect on Jesus' preferred address for God: our Father.

First, note that Jesus does not say, "*My* Father in heaven." The plural "our" reveals communion or fellowship with Jesus and our common Father in heaven, revealing "an entirely new relationship."[17] Jesus is communicating something profound regarding God's being and our relationship with God. Moreover, Jesus affirms our connection with him as brothers and sisters; Jesus' Father is our Father. Jesus wants us to share in his relationship with God the Father. He wants us to know that God loves us even as God has loved him (John 17:23). We need reminding of this mystery.

On the day of our baptism, we were adopted and "reborn" as sons and daughters of God.[18] By virtue of our baptism, we are invited to participate in God's being. The Blessed Trinity—one God, one indivisible unity of three persons, Father, Son, and Holy Spirit, working together to create, redeem, and sanctify—calls us to reproduce the pattern, the "mutual indwelling" of love, the intimate relationships, we find in God's being. To experience this profound level of love, Jesus invites us to address God as Father. What does this mean for us? Does it mean God is male? To gain a deepened understanding of this mystery, let us consider magisterial teaching found in the *Catechism of the Catholic Church*:

> By calling God "Father," the language of faith indicates two main things: that God is the first origin of everything and transcendent authority; and that he is at the same time goodness and loving care for all his children. God's parental tenderness can also be expressed by the image of motherhood, which emphasizes God's

immanence, the intimacy between Creator and creature. The language of faith thus draws on the human experience of parents, who are in a way the first representatives of God for man. But this experience also tells us that human parents are fallible and can disfigure the face of fatherhood and motherhood. We ought therefore to recall that God transcends the human distinction between the sexes. *He is neither man nor woman: he is God.* He also transcends human fatherhood and motherhood, although he is their origin and standard: no one is father as God is Father.[19]

Although sacred scripture includes feminine *and* masculine imagery to capture God's love and activity in the world,[20] the Catechism reminds us that language cannot exhaust the mystery of God. Even though we address God as Father, our understanding of God as Father is not to be limited by our understanding or experience of earthly parenting, especially when it is flawed and chaotic. Someone may have had a difficult relationship with an earthly parent, thereby making it challenging to understand God using parental language. They may not have experienced perfect love in their home environment. Perhaps one way of remedying this dilemma is by reminding the faithful that God is love: "So we have known and believe the love that God has for us. God is love, and those who abide in love abide in God, and God abides in them" (1 John 4:16).

We are called to stay in a relationship—to abide—with God. Consequently, St. John the Evangelist is communicating a mystery: those who stay constant in their loving will remain close to God, because God is love. Besides, God became one of us so that we can be like him (1 John 3:2). Jesus, assuming our humanity, humbled himself to be born as a baby. This tender moment is captured in the beautiful painting *Song of the Angels* by William-Adolphe Bouguereau. A print of this painting was donated to St. Augustine's Seminary in Scarborough, Ontario, Canada, where I teach, in 2012. I was gifted the donated print by a colleague on the day I facilitated a retreat on the theme of God's love, reflecting on the biblical truth that God so loved the world that he gave his only Son for us and our salvation (John 3:16). Jesus became one of us, choosing to live like us, laugh and cry like us, suffer and die like us, not using his divine powers for personal gain (Philippians 2:6).

When I brought the print home, I noticed a signature on the back: "From Father Love." Father Albert Love, a now deceased priest of the Archdiocese of Toronto, had donated the print to the seminary. Smiling with great joy and awe, I realized that Father Love's signature was a beautiful affirmation of the day's theme, a reminder that God is love and we are called to reflect God's love, remaining constant in our loving. I believe God was communicating something profound, encouraging us to address him and understand him as "Father Love." Experiencing profound love is a foretaste of heaven, reminding us, as Jesus taught, of "Our Father in heaven." Some may ask, however, "What is heaven?" or "Where is heaven?"

The Catechism describes the state of heaven as "this perfect life with the Most Holy Trinity — this communion of life and love with the Trinity, with the Virgin Mary, the angels and all the blessed … Heaven is the ultimate end and fulfilment of the deepest human longings, the state of supreme, definitive happiness."[21] We are reminded that heaven is not to be understood as a place or space, but rather "a way of being."[22] Pope Saint John Paul II, in his catechesis on heaven, explains that we can experience a foretaste of this state of perfect love when we participate in the sacramental life of the Church, especially the reception of the Eucharist and in loving our neighbour.[23] Moreover, we experience a foretaste when we do God's will and are surrounded by others who do the same.

When we follow the two great commandments, "You shall love the Lord your God with all your heart, and with all your soul, and with all your mind" and "You shall love your neighbour as yourself" (Matthew 22:36-40),[24] we remain close to God and experience a foretaste of heaven, for as Pope John Paul II taught, heaven "is neither an abstraction nor a physical place in the clouds, but a living, personal relationship with the Holy Trinity."[25] This means God is ever present and accessible, especially when we give and receive love. St. Teresa of Avila emphasized this point when she spoke of the "little heaven" of our souls, where "the

Creator of heaven and earth dwells."[26] Heaven, she concludes, "is where God dwells."[27]

The more we love God, self, and others, the more we advance in holiness, for "Whoever does not love does not know God, for God is love ... There is no fear in love, but perfect love casts out fear; for fear has to do with punishment, and whoever fears has not reached perfection in love" (1 John 4:8, 18). St. Augustine, reflecting on this teaching, was aware that increasing love in relationships decreases the power of fear, so that we are not overcome by it.[28] There is no fear in heaven, only love, for God wills our flourishing for our own sake,[29] thereby desiring union with us. Jesus teaches us that God in heaven desires that we experience the joys of heaven, including the fruits of the Holy Spirit: "love, joy, peace, patience, kindness, generosity, faithfulness, gentleness, and self-control" (Galatians 5:22-23).

Our Father in heaven, then, could be understood as Our Father in love, for God's being is love in perfect form, free from fear or disordered attachments, a state of perfect bliss. This concurs with a private revelation received by a 19th-century religious sister in France:

> There is happiness, always new and such, it would seem, as never been enjoyed. It is a torrent of joy which flows unceasingly over the elect. Heaven is above all and beyond all—God: God loved, God relished, God delighted in; in one word, it is to be satisfied with God without ever being satisfied.[30]

The state of heaven, as described by this mystic, is the state where one reaches perfection in love, where one experiences union with God, and other souls in heaven, with joy overflowing. How does one attain such a state? The Holy Spirit, the power of God's love, assists us with the grace we need to learn how to love well and without fear. Sadly, however, some people have been set up in life to be less free, without having experienced unconditional love, not learning or knowing how to love well.

We Need the Father's Love

With so much existential angst, people are challenged to ponder the meaning of life, including questions around their identity (Who am

I?); community (To whom and with whom do I belong?); and purpose (How can I use my gifts and qualifications to magnify God and to grow in holiness?). The COVID-19 pandemic and other world issues have left us thinking about our existence and our future. Lockdowns, fuelling more and more isolation and loneliness, reminded us of the importance of connection and relationships. Well before the pandemic, there existed well-established research on the harm caused by isolation and loneliness. Dr. John T. Cacioppo and William Patrick, in their book *Loneliness: Human Nature and the Need for Social Connection*, document the effects of prolonged isolation. Loneliness, they found, is harder on the body than smoking, drinking, and obesity![31] Let that sink in. Consequently, after several periods of lockdown, reports of increased drug overdoses,[32] eating disorders, and suicide attempts and completions left families and communities reeling, thereby revealing death by despair.[33] In February 2023, the Centre for Disease Control (CDC) shared findings from a Youth Risk Behavior Survey completed by 17,000 adolescents across the United States in the fall of 2021, reporting that nearly three in five teenage girls experienced persistent and consistent depressing thoughts, and one in three considered suicide.[34]

The fallout exposed the fragile state of humanity, especially in families where there was pre-existing chaos. Internal chaos fuels external chaos. Unemployment, isolation, and disconnection from family and co-workers, coupled with other pre-existing factors such as poverty and abuse, left families feeling more and more vulnerable. Changes in behaviour were noticed and documented, showing how a culture of fear lowers our ability to reason, placing further limits on emotional freedom.[35]

Elsewhere, I examined some of the factors that influence human behaviour:[36]

* Family of origin issues/environment
* Prenatal care (maternal and paternal)
* Postnatal nurture

* Genetics

* Grace

Although it is beyond the scope of this short section in this book to offer a more fulsome discussion on the need for love and nurture, research reveals something we have known intuitively: love forms the child and informs their sense of identity. Most importantly, the person with a formed conscience who can reason, love, and feel remorse and empathy can overcome certain obstacles with the help of God's grace.[37] Accordingly, love helps us to self-regulate and to reason with freedom. While nature, including genetics or heritable traits, contributes to the formation of our personality, nurture is just as influential, including the time in the womb.[38]

The child needs to feel love, prenatally and postnatally, to thrive, free from exposure to environmental toxins, including pesticides, alcohol, and other substances.[39] Still other scholars document the harmful effects of maternal trauma, impacting fetal brain development:[40] "If the caregiver is in a highly dysregulated state, you will get cortisol passing through the placenta in utero, and this is now going to negatively impact whatever structures are evolving at that time."[41]

Children, Dr. Gabor Maté observes, "need attuned non-stressed emotionally available caregivers."[42] Sadly, there are children who are exposed to traumatic experiences, including the pain of their parents. For these individuals, trauma may have been experienced as "the response to a deeply distressing or disturbing event that overwhelms an individual's ability to cope, causes feelings of helplessness, diminishes their sense of self and their ability to feel the full range of emotions and experiences."[43] Access to trauma-informed education can assist with deepening our understanding of the harmful effects of trauma. This involves an understanding of what trauma means, including vicarious trauma, where someone witnesses or observes the trauma experienced by another person.

To help us discern whether trauma has occurred, Dr. Maté prepared a checklist to assist those who are open to examining their emotional responses to painful situations. He says,

> It is not trauma if the following remain true over the long term:
>
> -It does not limit you, constrict you, diminish your capacity to feel or think or to trust or assert yourself, to experience suffering without succumbing to despair or to witness it with compassion.
>
> -It does not keep you from holding your pain and sorrow and fear without being overwhelmed and without having to escape habitually into work or compulsive self-soothing or self-stimulating by whatever means.
>
> -You are not left compelled either to aggrandize yourself or to efface yourself for the sake of gaining acceptance or to justify your existence.
>
> -It does not impair your capacity to experience gratitude for the beauty and wonder of life.[44]

Sadly, trauma can impact a child's development. Left untreated, the person risks becoming a caregiver or parent with unresolved trauma, unintentionally contributing to a child's inability to attach and possibly leading to feelings of disassociation.[45] Negatively impacting relationships, the harmful experiences can become a cycle, repeated in future generations. Conversely, the love and nurture expressed by loving parents decreases the possibility of at-risk behaviour in adolescent males and females. The first three to seven years, commonly referred to as the "fourth trimester," especially if there is a stable home environment and nurture, contribute to a child's well-being, helping them to self-regulate, thereby reducing at-risk behaviour.[46] Whether it is maternal trauma or postnatal trauma, it changes us. We need accompaniment and comfort, including access to material and spiritual resources, and possibly therapy, to recover.

Jesus, fully human and fully divine, with his infused knowledge, knows the importance of consistent love and nurture. By addressing and knowing God as Father, he is communicating how God's love is needed, especially to compensate for pain caused by early deficits in the parent–child relationship. Harriet McCarthy's research on early neglect and abandonment supports this insight. Having studied almost 300 school-age children who had experienced trauma and severe neglect, she documented problems with learning, attachment issues, delayed formation of conscience, and oppositional behaviour.[47] Addressing God as Father, our loving parent, signals our openness to being parented or reparented by our God who is love.

Greg Anderson, a man who experienced great healing, was comforted through his meditation on the Lord's Prayer. In his writing on cancer and the Lord's Prayer, he encourages us to "stop saying 'Our Father' on Sunday, only to spend the rest of the week living like an orphan."[48] How many people live their day-to-day lives this way? Many years ago, my dear friend shared her pain of missing her parents. They had been deceased for a while. She was married, with four adult children, but she felt alone and orphaned. She missed being someone's daughter.

I, too, miss being someone's daughter. It's been over thirty years since my father passed and over twenty years since my mother passed. No matter how old we are, we need to feel connected and loved. The good news, however, is even though we may be adults, parents, or grandparents, God continues to parent us, and if we remain open to conversion and healing, God will direct our path and teach us how to be like him. Thankfully, God continues to raise me, directing my actions and helping me in my discernment. The key is to maintain a state of intimacy with God, including awareness of God's activity in our lives, and pay close attention to our surroundings, whether we are being loving and truthful in all our actions. God, honouring our free will, waits for us to respond to his offer of assistance, his grace or free gift of strengthening. As Jesus promised, our "burden" can be lightened (Matthew 11:30) when we approach him and remain open to God's assistance.

Parenting can be very demanding, especially where there is a lack of resources and support from extended family and friends. Well-documented cases from Brazil, for example, reveal the great challenge of raising children in underprivileged communities. Having witnessed the struggle many women face when they are abandoned by their husbands, many grandparents step in to help their daughters raise their children.[49] The challenge of raising children alone, without emotional and spiritual support, can make matters worse. A recent report from Statistics Canada shows that the percentage of children aged 0 to 14 living with one parent is about 19.2 percent.[50] An earlier study found that children raised in single-parent homes, especially if supports were lacking and access to the other parent was limited or non-existent, face increased risk of emotional, behavioural, academic, and social problems.[51] This finding does not suggest that single parents are worse parents; rather, the challenge of juggling parental, social, economic, and personal responsibilities makes it more difficult to meet children's needs. If we add a painful divorce, death of a spouse, illness, abandonment, abuse, or experience of poverty, the stress levels increase substantially.

Whether a two-parent home or a single-parent home, families become vulnerable whenever financial, medical, or emotional hardship hits. When one person suffers, the whole family feels it. When both spouses are suffering, it may be difficult to reach out to the other, because the strength and emotional stamina needed in such situations may be lacking. Remaining close to God in prayer, and open to God's providence, relieves the burden and strengthens us to endure the many challenges that come our way. This is evident in scripture. The deeper meaning of the account of the Wedding at Cana (John 2:1-11), for example, communicates the transformation that occurs when Jesus, consubstantial with the Father, is invited to help, heal, and strengthen marriages and families. Our God who is heaven and in heaven loves us so much that he wants us to share in his being.

There are many spiritual insights that God wants us to experience here and now, giving us a sneak preview of the heavenly state. While time on earth can never capture the glory of heaven, God wants to give us some of the spiritual riches of heaven so we can grow, heal, and prepare for greater glory. The scriptures remind us of those heavenly insights that can be gained on earth:

Surely, this commandment that I am commanding you today is not too hard for you, nor is it too far away. It is not in heaven, that you should say, "Who will go up to heaven for us, and get it for us so that we may hear it and observe it?" Neither is it beyond the sea, that you should say, "Who will cross over to the other side of the sea for us, and get it for us so that we may hear it and observe it?" No, the word is very near to you; it is in your mouth and in your heart for you to observe. (Deuteronomy 30:11-14)

This passage reminds us that God's truths are accessible to us, preparing us for transformation and final glory. Encouragingly, there are truths that can be learned and pondered, serving as a preparation for heaven, a state of union with God. Moreover, we are reassured of God's closeness because his Word is present within us, ready to be observed.

The first line of the Lord's Prayer is an invitation to accept God as Father Love, acknowledging heaven as a state or way of being with God. The seven petitions that follow provide the road map or assistance—or, as Pope Francis says—the "life programme" for Jesus' disciples, guiding us toward this heavenly state.

I did not realize then, as I do now, that a King of such Majesty dwelt within the small palace of my soul. Otherwise, it seems to me that I could never possibly have left him alone so often. At least, from time to time, I should have remained in his company, and should have watched with greater care that this palace be not tarnished.[52]

Reflection Questions

- ▸ What is your understanding of God?
- ▸ Are your images of God positive or negative? In what way? How can you start to revise or challenge any negative ones?
- ▸ Can you relate to the address of God as "Father"/parent? How? If not, how can you begin to see God in this way?
- ▸ Have you invited God's "fatherly care" into your home and family? If yes, how? If not, how could you do this?

PRAYER

Loving God,
we thank you for calling us your children.
We thank you for Jesus, our Saviour and elder brother.
Grant that we may learn to parent and love each other
with the love Jesus shared with you.
May wisdom, patience, and endurance
be with all those who seek your will and guidance.
Amen.

Petition #1

Hallowed be your name

Bless the Lord, O my soul, and all that is within me, bless his
holy name.
Bless the Lord, O my soul, and do not forget all his benefits—
who forgives all your iniquity, who heals all your diseases,
who redeems your life from the Pit, who crowns you with
steadfast love and mercy,
who satisfies you with good as long as you live
so that your youth is renewed like the eagle's.
(Psalm 103:1-5)

While we begin the Lord's Prayer by recognizing God our "Father," whose presence is boundless and universal, the first petition, echoing the instruction found in the first commandment that "you shall have no other gods before me" (Exodus 20:3), calls us to take our worship to the next level by honouring God's name. The verb "to hallow" speaks of adoration, praise, and thanksgiving; in other words, we are to acknowledge the holiness of God's name by adoring and praising God always and everywhere. Spoken of throughout the scriptures, the holiness of God's name is affirmed throughout; for example, according to a vision of the prophet Isaiah, seraphs, who were in attendance above the Lord, called to one another and said: "Holy, holy, holy, is the Lord of hosts; the whole earth is full of his glory" (Isaiah 6:3). Moreover, harkening back to our days of preparation for the Sacrament of Confirmation, there is a gift of the Holy Spirit associated with this act of reverence—the fear of the Lord, or wonder and awe (Isaiah 11:2).

Dr. Dacher Keltner, an expert in the science of human emotion, is a professor of psychology at the University of California, Berkeley. His book, *Awe: The New Science of Everyday Wonder and How It Can Transform Your Life*, is a bestseller. He describes awe as "the feeling of being in the presence of something vast that transcends your current understanding of the world."[1] As religion's central emotion, awe, he says, leads to joy and bliss. Having studied the writings of mystics across many generations and having interviewed people from around the world, he discovered that we must be more intentional regarding the search for moments of awe, including the appreciation of "moral beauty." It sounds like Keltner is tapping into our understanding of the transcendentals or properties of God's being: truth, goodness, and beauty. Honouring God signals that we are "in the presence of something vast that transcends" our "current understanding of the world." The awe is so intense, it has been challenging to capture or exhaust this feeling using words or names for God. Still, the way in which we honour God using various names signals our reverence and intent.

Apart from *Abba* Father, God is known by other names. A few examples include:

* Mighty One (Genesis 1:1)
* The Living One who sees me (Genesis 16:13)
* God Almighty (Genesis 17:1)
* I AM (Exodus 3:13-15)
* Lord (1 Samuel 24:8)

Jesus is also known by other names. Here are some examples:

* Christ (Anointed/Messiah) of God (Luke 9:20)
* Word (John 1:1)
* Son of God (Matthew 2:15)
* Lamb of God (John 1:29)
* Immanuel (Isaiah 7:14)
* Holy One of God (Mark 1:24)

* Good Shepherd (John 10:11)
* Bread of Life (John 6:35)
* Alpha and Omega (Revelation 1:8)
* New Adam (1 Corinthians 15:45)
* Lord (John 20:28)

Names matter. In the biblical world, names hold meaning, often revealing someone's identity.[2] Since we cannot exhaust the mystery of God's being using language, various names have been revealed to help us understand and know God with greater intimacy. Jesus, whose name means "God saves," shares in the honour showed his Father's name.

Jesus, our Saviour, is the source of our salvation (Hebrews 5:9-10). Accordingly, understanding the deeper meaning of salvation helps us to appreciate what God does for us and in us through Jesus Christ. Salvation or divine health[3] is a gift associated with the following:

* Rescue from the dangers in this life/deliverance from evil (Matthew 8:23-27)
* Final entry into heaven (1 Corinthians 3:15)
* Forgiveness of sins (Luke 1:77)
* Health and healing (Luke 8:48)
* Conversion (Luke 19:1-10)

Simeon, described as a righteous and devout man, "would not see death before he had seen the Lord's Messiah" (Luke 2:26). When Mary and Joseph bring the infant Jesus to the temple, Simeon takes the baby into his arms and says, "Master, now you are dismissing your servant in peace, according to your word; for my eyes have seen your salvation, which you have prepared in the presence of all peoples, a light for revelation to the Gentiles and for glory to your people." Simeon saw salvation in Jesus Christ. In other words, he saw the restoration of humanity and all creation in Jesus. Jesus' name revealed his mission: to deliver, forgive, heal, and transform God's people, preparing them for everlasting life in heaven and reconciliation with God. Honouring God's name is part of this process.

St. Paul, in his beautiful Christological hymn found in his letter
to the Philippians, reminds us that God exalted Jesus, giving him "the
name that is above every name, so that at the name of Jesus every knee
should bend, in heaven and on earth and under the earth, and every
tongue should confess that Jesus Christ is Lord, to the glory of God the
Father" (2:9-11). Sadly, however, too many times Jesus' name has not
been honoured: it has been taken in vain in movies, on social media,
and in everyday conversation. The Psalmist refers to those who speak
of God "maliciously" (Psalm 139:20), indicating a dark, malevolent intent whenever the Lord's name is used. Elsewhere, the Psalmist writes,
"How long, O God, is the foe to scoff? Is the enemy to revile your name
forever?" (Psalm 74:10).

Whenever we use the Lord's name, we are called to examine our
intent or motivation. The energy we attach to words matters. Dr. Larry
Dossey, author of *Healing Words: The Power of Prayer and the Practice
of Medicine*, documents the fruitful outcome associated with positive,
loving intent. Conversely, he documents the negative outcome associated with dark and malicious intent.[4] How can we expect to receive
God's blessing when we dishonour God's name with reckless and hostile
intent? Apart from Dr. Dossey, who has collected peer-reviewed data
to support his claims, I have encountered some people who have made
the act of blasphemy habitual, yielding anecdotal evidence regarding
the connection between habitual blasphemy and dark, chaotic lives.
Blasphemy signals that we reject God's favour, that we refuse to be like
God. Instead, honouring God requires disciplined speech.

A saying attributed to Rumi, a Persian mystic who lived from 1207
to 1273, suggests that our speech must pass through three gates: Is it
true? Is it kind? Is it necessary? Similarly, countless proverbs and other
scriptural verses warn against harmful speech. Jesus says, "I tell you, on
the day of judgment you will have to give an account of every careless
word you utter; for by your words you will be justified, and by your
words you will be condemned" (Matthew 12:36-37). We cannot ask
God for help in one breath and curse God and our brothers and sisters
in the next. Cursing counteracts and prevents God's blessing. The Lord's

Prayer, however, calls us to honour God with our minds, hearts, actions, and words, following God's ways always and everywhere.

Jesus, in Matthew's gospel, reminds us to "[b]e perfect, therefore, as your heavenly Father is perfect" (5:48). Reading this verse in context (Matthew 5:43-48), "perfect" not only means completeness but also loving as God loves, without partiality. In other words, Jesus is calling us to be like God, since the experience of salvation is associated with a desire to be with God. Magnanimity is the great virtue acquired in the process, demonstrating how we strive for excellence, avoiding the temptation to magnify our mistakes. Instead, we magnify God, striving always to be like God, loving like God. Honouring God's name, with all our thoughts, words, and actions, helps us to strive for holiness or completeness. St. Peter Chrysologus, an early Church father, makes this connection for us:

> We ask God to hallow his name, which by its own holiness saves and makes holy all creation … It is this name that gives salvation to a lost world. But we ask that this name of God should be hallowed in us through our actions. For God's name is blessed when we live well, but is blasphemed when we live wickedly. As the Apostle says: "The name of God is blasphemed among the Gentiles because of you." We ask then that, just as the name of God is holy, so we may obtain his holiness in our souls.[5]

God's own holiness desires to be united with our holiness. True union with God happens when we give back to God the image God gave us—in its original state.[6] Hence, it is worthwhile to revisit what it means to be created in God's image.[7] To be created in God's image means we participate in God's being, possessing the following:[8]

* Dignity of the person (we are made up of body and soul)[9]
* Capacity for self-knowledge/self-awareness
* Capacity for self-possession or self-control/self-mastery (a virtue and a fruit of the Spirit)
* Capacity for self-determination or free will

* Capacity/freedom to enter into relationship with others
* Capacity/freedom to accept God's grace, responding in faith and love, without fear

Although we are created in God's image, we need God's grace to be like God.[10] We need God's grace to work on our souls so that our intellect and free will can be used to reason properly, reflecting the "mind of Christ" (1 Corinthians 2:16). This is the process of divinization, the process of becoming like God. This means we must respond to God's grace and cooperate with God's plan to enhance these God-given capacities with which we have been endowed. We become more and more like God when we sense an increase in self-knowledge and self-awareness, an increase in self-mastery, and the freedom to love and reason without imagined fear. The likeness of God is restored in us when we have achieved "perfection in divine love."[11]

God's grace can act on our souls when we cooperate with God, indicating our desire to experience communion with God. For Christians, this involves carrying out our promises to follow the commandments, living our baptismal promises, and loving God, self, and others. No doubt, these actions contribute to our sanctification. As we become more and more self-aware—of our thoughts, words, deeds, and choices—we should be moving closer and closer to thoughts, words, deeds, and choices, and to relationships that are fulfilling and life-giving. This inner transformation will fuel the process of sanctification, and our lives will give God the glory that is desired. St. Paul, aware of this process in his own life, had the inspiration to write: "May the God of peace himself sanctify you entirely; and may your spirit and soul and body be kept sound [complete] and blameless at the coming of our Lord Jesus Christ" (1 Thessalonians 5:23). The whole person is involved in the process of sanctification, or the call to holiness.

The first petition, honouring God's holy name, invites us to consider our own call to holiness, a topic that was heavily emphasized in the teaching of the bishops at the Second Vatican Council:

The Church, whose mystery is being set forth by this Sacred Synod, is believed to be indefectibly holy. Indeed Christ, the Son of God, who with the Father and the Spirit is praised as "uniquely holy," loved the Church as His bride, delivering Himself up for her. He did this that He might sanctify her. He united her to Himself as His own body and brought it to perfection by the gift of the Holy Spirit for God's glory. Therefore in the Church, everyone whether belonging to the hierarchy, or being cared for by it, is called to holiness, according to the saying of the Apostle: "For this is the will of God, your sanctification". However, this holiness of the Church is unceasingly manifested, and must be manifested, in the fruits of grace which the Spirit produces in the faithful; it is expressed in many ways in individuals, who in their walk of life, tend toward the perfection of charity, thus causing the edification of others; in a very special way this (holiness) appears in the practice of the counsels, customarily called "evangelical." This practice of the counsels, under the impulsion of the Holy Spirit, undertaken by many Christians, either privately or in a Church-approved condition or state of life, gives and must give in the world an outstanding witness and example of this same holiness.[12]

The official teaching of the Church calls all people, regardless of state of life, to holiness. Sadly, some Christians may be under the false impression that God calls a select few to be holy, namely clergy and religious. Our state of life, as we are aware, does not guarantee holiness. It is our will to be made holy, helped by God's grace that brings about the process of sanctification. A wise priest from Toronto once said to a group of young men discerning the priesthood, "Pray that God will lead you to the state of life through which he can squeeze the most out of you." No doubt, for many it will be the state of marriage, while for others it will be the single state, or Holy Orders for men, or religious life for some men and women. Apart from our state of life, our profession, if we find ourselves serving in a certain sector, can be used as an instrument, where we use our gifts and qualifications to evangelize so we can witness to the power of God's love in our lives.

Sacramental baptism, making us adopted sons and daughters of God, contains and confers the grace we need to start the process of sanctification. As we develop our faith life, reaching a certain level of spiritual maturity, we begin to follow and trust the promptings of the Holy Spirit, showing us the way toward vocations, professions, and relationships that are life-giving. Step by step, the Holy Spirit reveals those aspects of our behaviour in need of pruning or elimination altogether, but we must be open to this process. It is this process that will contribute to the building of God's kingdom on earth—our next petition.

Reflection Questions

> ‣ How do you show honour to God's name?
> ‣ How do you live out your call to holiness? In your family? In the workplace? As a volunteer?

PRAYER

Creator God,
we praise your holy name and rejoice
in your great love for us.
Grant that our words, thoughts,
and actions are disciplined
so that we may glorify your holy name
with our entire being.
We ask this through Christ our Lord.
Amen.

"Your greatest contribution to the kingdom of God may not be something you do but someone you raise."

—Andy Stanley, Twitter, April 17, 2013

Petition #2

Your kingdom come

For the kingdom of God is not food and drink but righteousness and peace and joy in the Holy Spirit. (Romans 14:17)

W hat is God's kingdom or reign like? Summarizing teaching found in scripture, the Catechism teaches that "thy kingdom come" refers "primarily to the final coming of the reign of God through Christ's return."[1] Although this suggests that the kingdom of God is in the state of approaching, the "Kingdom of God has been coming since the Last Supper and, in the Eucharist, it is in our midst...."[2] God's kingdom, then, represents a state of already/ not yet, a common expression used in eschatology, or the theological study of the last things, namely, death, heaven, hell, and purgatory. Redemption was accomplished in Jesus Christ but is in the state of being completed in us, the members of his Body. When we receive the Eucharist and cooperate with God's grace, the kingdom of God feels nearby. It is a state in which the fruits of the Spirit (Galatians 5:22-23) are present, infusing our thoughts and actions with love and wisdom, inspiring relationships and communities.

The second petition speaks of the arrival of God's reign on earth, where, according to St. Paul, "righteousness and peace and joy in the Holy Spirit" will be enjoyed. In his letter to Titus, Paul writes:

For the grace of God has appeared, bringing salvation to all, training us to renounce impiety and worldly passions, and in the present age to live lives that are self-controlled, upright and godly, while we wait for the blessed hope and the manifestation of the glory of our great God and Saviour, Jesus Christ. He it is who gave himself for us that he might redeem us from all iniquity and purify for himself a people of his own who are zealous for good deeds. (2:11-14)

Paul knows we have been equipped with God's grace, preparing us for the kingdom of God to come in glory. It is our responsibility, however, to work toward the coming of God's reign with right action and right thought, working in accord with the Spirit, and producing the fruits of the Spirit. We experience the coming of the kingdom in degrees of glory, starting with greater self-awareness, self-knowledge, and self-control.

St. Paul tracks this process and documents his experience of it with two passages, in two letters, revealing the beginning of the process, when things seem dim, and the final stages of the process, when there is greater clarity, wherein we come to mirror Christ, being more and more like him:

For now we see in a mirror, dimly, but then we will see face to face. Now I know only in part; then I will know fully, even as I have been fully known. (1 Corinthians 13:12)

And all of us, with unveiled faces, seeing the glory of the Lord as though reflected in a mirror, are being transformed into the same image from one degree of glory to another; for this comes from the Lord, the Spirit. (2 Corinthians 3:18)

Similarly, St. John the Evangelist, reminding us that we are children of God, is aware of this process of transformation:

See what love the Father has given us, that we should be called children of God; and that is what we are ... Beloved, we are God's children now; what we will be has not yet been revealed. What we do know is this: when he is revealed, we will be like him, for we will see him as he is. And all who have this hope in him purify themselves, just as he is pure. (1 John 3:1-3)

John is summarizing the main insights of the first two petitions, including the opening verse of the Lord's Prayer, affirming God as our Father. Honouring God involves knowing God, and striving for God's kingdom involves transformation and the renewal of relationships. Although the kingdom of heaven is experienced as a state of transformation infused with the fruits of the Spirit, it also consists of life-giving relationships—individuals and other heavenly creatures who do God's will—for perfection in love involves union with God and others, a teaching made clear by Jesus.

Jesus, announcing the coming of the kingdom, identifies John the Baptist as one of the great prophets, "yet the least in the kingdom of heaven is greater than he" (Matthew 11:11). He then goes on to say something unusual: "From the days of John the Baptist until now the kingdom of heaven has suffered violence, and the violent take it by force" (Matthew 11:12). What does this mean? It sounds like the kingdom of heaven is being attacked by violent people. Some scholars believe that "suffered violence" is a bad translation. A better translation includes more context, showing how since the time of John the Baptist, with so many people gathering to hear his message and others who, due to his message, are now seeking Jesus, people are eager to experience the kingdom because they are actively searching for it and desiring to take hold of it.

A simple search using a concordance shows that the Greek *harpazousin*, a variant of the word *harpazo*, translated as "suffered violence," is more accurately understood as to seize, catch up, or snatch away. Similarly, the Greek *biastes*, translated as "the violent," is more accurately understood as "one in eager pursuit." In context, what is being communicated here is the hunger and thirst people have for the kingdom of God; all that was needed was someone to announce its arrival, thereby giving hope to those who have been waiting, some with great discouragement.

Whether it is the teaching of Jesus or the transformative experiences of St. John the Baptist, or St. Paul, what is being communicated is that we are being prepared for the glory of God to enter our lives. This involves preparation and discipline on our part. To be sure, this can be difficult and demanding. Accordingly, we need God's assistance to permeate every aspect of our lives. The daughter of Martin Luther King Jr. was once interviewed about the trials of the present day. Moved by her strong faith, she said that we cannot shut God out of our public lives and ask God to intervene in only part of our lives. God's kingdom is experienced when God's ways are welcome in the workplace, in the family, and in all areas of our community.

One of my theology professors, Ovey Mohammed SJ (1933–2020), once said in class that for God's kingdom to come, ours must go: "Your kingdom come, my kingdom go!" This view suggests the need for greater self-awareness and ongoing conversion, including the transformation of communities. The kingdom of God as a state, then, "does not refer here to a territory but to the divine power and authority that now is in the world, transforming the old into new, the unjust into just, and sickness into health."[3] Messianic prophecy led some to believe that the coming Messiah would establish a new territory, suggesting a more militarized approach. Instead, the kingdom of God, this state of union with God as explained by Jesus, involves a process of growth:

> "The kingdom of heaven is like a mustard seed that someone took and sowed in his field; it is the smallest of all seeds, but when it has grown it is the greatest of shrubs and becomes a tree, so that the birds of the air come and make nests in its branches. … The kingdom of heaven is like yeast that a woman took and mixed in with three measures of flour until all of it was leavened." (Matthew 13:31-33)

This journey of growth began on the day of our baptism. Baptism, "as the basis of the whole Christian life," is the "gateway to life in the Spirit."[4] Baptismal grace nourishes the seeds of the kingdom that are found in individuals and communities. Inspired by God's grace, we strive to do God's will as we grow and become more responsible, sharing our gifts and inspiring others to seek out the kingdom. The more responsible we become, the more loving and compassionate our relationships, the more justice is present in families and communities, the more integrated we become, the more righteous and Christ-like we become, the more God's kingdom will be present here on earth. The process will change us cell by cell, so that just as a seed becomes a tree, we will reflect God's image and likeness more and more here on earth.

This reminds me of a story shared by a local artist. He described how artists in the 11th and 12th centuries purified gold. Their method included heating gold, glass, and sand, using very high temperatures, to separate out the gold. At first, the gold was extracted as gold dust. The purifying method was used to remove hidden impurities, causing them to rise to the surface with intense heat. The artisan then skimmed the impurities, resulting in clear liquid, so clear that the goldsmith could now see his reflection. Applying this method to the spiritual life, God's grace acts on our souls and with our cooperation makes us more and more like him. Divinization, as explained previously, is the term used to describe this process. We remain creatures, but we are like God. The words of the priest at the preparation of the gifts capture this mystery: "By the mystery of this water and wine may we come to share in the *divinity* of Christ who humbled himself to share in our humanity."[5]

Although the process is demanding, the glory we experience will surpass all understanding. Moreover, the good news is that research on the fruits of this journey reveals the benefits of faithful endurance. Elsewhere, I documented the findings of Patricia Treece, author of *The Sanctified Body*:

> Patricia Treece has studied the physiological and spiritual benefits that come with the call to holiness. Treece, an expert on 19th and 20th century saints and mystics, has spent eleven years researching the body in the sanctified state … The person is transformed at the psychological and spiritual level. Some of this transformation, she discovered, manifests itself at the physical level.[6]

This research shows that whole persons experience the fruits of the kingdom. Like the goldsmith who refines gold using a delicate process, God's grace refines us, welcoming us into his kingdom. Accordingly, the body, too, benefits from this process.[7] No doubt, however, our pursuit of this kingdom process will involve different phases or seasons: seasons of drought and seasons of plenty. Seasons of drought may bring times of struggle related to loss, grief, pain, illness, and sorrow. Seasons of plenty may bring times of joy, hope, restoration, and peace. While we grow in both seasons, we are called to be hopeful in seasons of drought and thankful and prepared in seasons of plenty. An abrupt change of season can happen at any time. It is not a matter of if but when. When this occurs, we may find ourselves experiencing time differently. For the persons experiencing drought, time may seem to drag: hours feel long, leaving us with thoughts of dread. Conversely, seasons of plenty seem to go too fast: five hours delighting in a first date feel like minutes. These precious moments are a foretaste of heaven, a state of timelessness, where the kingdom of God feels near.

The good news is that God's grace does not disappoint us (see Romans 5:5). Regardless of season, we are strengthened and encouraged, especially by other faithful pilgrims who have travelled before us. St. Paul, sharing his own struggles, was reminded by our Lord, "My grace is sufficient for you, for power is made perfect in weakness" (2 Corinthians 12:9). St. Paul learns that with God's grace, we will not be overcome by vulnerabilities or seasons of drought. He comes to understand that peace, a fruit of the Spirit, is not the absence of adversity; rather, it is the presence of God's anointing and power—the presence that "surpasses all understanding" (Philippians 4:7).

Eventually, once the kingdom of God is fully alive in us, we shall become like Jesus—the evergreen tree, keeping its green colour all year long. Regardless of the season, God's grace keeps us steady and hopeful. The more we nurture the seed with the supernatural or infused virtues— *faith*: the habit of believing, knowing, and trusting God (Hebrews 11:1); *hope*: the habit of waiting with joy, patience, and perseverance (Romans 12:12); and *charity*: the habit of loving (1 Corinthians 13:1-13)—like the yeast, with the help of God's grace, we will cause God's kingdom to grow within us and in our communities. Nevertheless, we must desire the kingdom within ourselves before we see it alive in our surroundings:

"So if anyone is in Christ, there is a new creation: everything old has passed away; see, everything has become new!" (2 Corinthians 5:17).

Just as Paul understood Jesus as the New Adam (1 Corinthians 15:45), as a sneak preview of God in his divinity and a sneak preview of humanity in its original state before the Fall, we must remember the good news that we are called to be made new. I tell my students that while I am not the "New Josephine," I am *becoming* the "New Josephine." Bit by bit, God's grace works on our souls, as we are transformed for the better. Once we become like God, we experience God's kingdom in its full glory. Accordingly, our desire to experience the kingdom of God inspires us to do God's will, the next petition.

> For this reason, since the day we heard it, we have not ceased praying for you and asking that you may be filled with the knowledge of God's will in all spiritual wisdom and understanding, so that you may lead lives worthy of the Lord, fully pleasing to him, as you bear fruit in every good work and as you grow in knowledge of God. May you be made strong with all the strength that comes from his glorious power, and may you be prepared to endure everything with patience, while joyfully giving thanks to the Father, who has enabled you to share in the inheritance of the saints in the light. He has rescued us from the power of darkness and transferred us into the kingdom of his beloved Son, in whom we have redemption, the forgiveness of sins. (Colossians 1:9-14)

Reflection Questions

> ‣ What is your understanding of God's kingdom? Is it something we can experience in the present?
>
> ‣ Have you invited God's kingdom into your family, your workplace, your community?
>
> ‣ What needs to happen for your community to be a foretaste of God's kingdom?

PRAYER

Merciful God,
you know our struggles.
You know those things that keep us
from being fulfilled in you.
Help us grow in love and understanding.
Give us the courage to seek your kingdom.
Grant that we may be open to
the transformation you will for us.
Amen.

Petition #3

Your will be done, on earth as it is in heaven

Trust in the Lord with all your heart,
and do not rely on your own insight.
In all your ways acknowledge him,
and he will make straight your paths.
(Proverbs 3:5-6)

Like the insight shared in the proverb found above, the prophet Jeremiah, speaking for God to the people, communicates the same need for trust in God: "For surely I know the plans I have for you, says the Lord, plans for your welfare and not for harm, to give you a future with hope" (Jeremiah 29:11). This scripture affirms that it is God's will that we flourish. The desire for us to experience the kingdom, the focus of the second petition, is strategically positioned before the third petition, that God's will be done on earth as it is in heaven. It is precisely this desire to taste the fruits of the kingdom that moves us to do God's will, mirroring the heavenly state in our earthly activities. The key, however, is knowing and doing God's will.

A person once asked a pastor, "How do we know what God's will is?" The pastor replied that we know God's will or God's intent for us through the teachings of the scriptures, most especially through what is known as revealed moral law. The Ten Commandments, for example, give us direction on how to conduct ourselves in our families and our communities.[1] Moreover, the fulfillment of these commandments leads to interior freedom: joy, peace, and ease. If a married person who is tempted to have an affair wonders what God's will is for this situation, consulting the commandments reveals the answer—adultery goes against God's will. Similarly, if someone is tempted to lie or steal, the commandments reveal that these actions are not compatible with God's will: not only because they are wrong and sinful, but also they have devastating consequences. Placing limits on our emotional freedom, the consequences reveal that the action is both wrong and sinful. God is revealing to us that there are divine and binding laws that are immutable or non-changing: these laws govern the consequences of human behaviour. For every act of theft or harm, there is a debt, meaning something was robbed from another, whether it be a person, a thing, or a state of joy. Is this freedom? Doing God's will, then, involves desiring balance and justice. Accordingly, God promises blessings for obeying the law (Deuteronomy 7:11-15). God's desire for order, not chaos, goes back to the first act of creation.

In the first creation account (Genesis 1:1-2), we hear that there was a "formless void" and "darkness" before God created the heavens and the earth. This suggests chaos and a dark emptiness. As part of God's act of creation, God brings light and order. What's more, God's love brings us, all creatures, and all creation into existence. The establishment of light or clarity and order paves the way for loving relationships to thrive. Consequently, doing God's will involves loving like God, remaining life-giving in all choices and actions. Jesus, fully human and fully God, imparts this wisdom throughout his teaching ministry.

Apart from the Ten Commandments, Jesus, after being asked "which commandment in the law is the greatest," responds by repeating two additional great commandments found in the Old Testament: "'You shall love the Lord your God with all your heart, and with all your soul, and with all your mind.' This is the greatest and first commandment. And a second is like it: 'You shall love your neighbour as yourself.' On these two commandments hang all the law and the prophets" (Matthew 22:36-40).[2] In other words, Jesus is saying that all other commandments or prophecy hinge on the fulfillment of these two commandments. The good news is that God created us with certain capacities to discern and know God's will. God, the source of eternal law, gives us guidance through two expressions of his moral law.[3]

We have already considered one expression of moral law: revealed law found in sacred scripture. Another expression of moral law, related to the first, is known as natural law. It is considered natural because it is part of human nature and includes our ability to reason, so that we can come to know the difference between "good and the evil, the truth and the lie."[4] This means that, regardless of religious affiliation, or the lack thereof, people were created to know the natural law. It provides a foundation for those who lack faith to discover and accept revealed law. Unchanging or immutable, the natural law is "written on [our] hearts" (Romans 2:15) because we are created in God's image. And as we have seen earlier, we are endowed with certain capacities. We can reason and discover moral truths because we were created to participate in God's being. This process of discovery is aided by God's grace because "the precepts of natural law are not perceived by everyone clearly and immediately."[5] God wants us to grow in wisdom, knowing moral and religious truths with certainty and clarity.[6]

We come to know religious and moral truths with the help of God's grace and through the study of sacred scripture and tradition, with faith giving us access to the mysteries of our faith, that which is unseen (Hebrews 11:1). Using our ability to reason, we can come to know foundational moral truths, including the observation and study of what is seen and experienced. This process is necessary, especially when another type of law, civil law, may be at odds with what God has revealed to us to be true and good. Something may be considered legal in one context but wrong and sinful according to the law that is in accord with God's will. Reason and faith, then, work together to help us know and accept God's will for our lives. Thankfully, we have been given guidance to help us seek that which is true and just. Church leaders are no exception to this process. Concerning governance, Church leaders are assisted by a code of ecclesiastical law, known as canon law: "a legal system, by which the Church lives for the just exercise of her sacred mission."[7] This, too, helps Church leaders to guide the faithful to know and discern the correct way forward with many ecclesiastical matters.

Nevertheless, Jesus affirmed the need to know the intent of the law, or to understand the purpose of the law, as opposed to limiting our understanding to following rules to avoid punishment. This is made clear when he says, "You have heard that it was said, 'You shall not commit adultery.' But I say to you that everyone who looks at a woman with lust has already committed adultery with her in his heart" (Matthew 5:27-28). In the time of Jesus, the punishment for adultery was death.[8] Jesus, as a Jew, knows this.

To help his followers understand what is known as the "spirit of the law," I believe he makes the following point about the intent of the law on adultery: Did you not commit adultery because you fear the consequences? Or did you not commit adultery because you *know* and *believe* it is wrong and sinful, thereby frustrating emotional and spiritual freedom? Moreover, he's making it clear that the intent or beginning of temptation begins in the mind. A person may not be engaging in a certain activity to avoid punishment, but their thoughts are contrary to God's will. A similar analogy includes following the rules of the road. Do we slow down in traffic out of fear of getting a speeding ticket? Or do we move at the speed limit to prevent accidents, the intent of the law? Our motivation to act or not to act should hinge on our understanding of the purpose or intent of the law. On our own, however, we may feel limited or tempted. No doubt, we need help and inspiration.

We need God's grace to assist us so that our ability to reason is strengthened, helping us to know the difference between right and wrong. As we develop our moral compass, we learn to follow certain laws, even though we may struggle with their purpose. With love and nurture, our conscience develops in response to this process. A life of grace, as St. Paul discovered, helps us to accept and obey God's will, knowing when we have strayed from God's purpose for our lives.[9] Accordingly, as our conscience forms, we come to feel remorse when we do not act according to God's will.[10] Sadly, at times, we may not trust

God's will for us. Like Adam and Eve, we may be tempted to believe we know better.

Adam and Eve were created in a state known as "original happiness or justice."[11] This is the state they experienced before original sin. Another defining feature of this state is "original innocence"—a time of trust and love, including the correct use of our bodies to glorify God.[12] Sadly, the account of the first sin (Genesis 3:1-24) reveals the source of what we call "original sin," namely, the illusion that we can find fulfillment and freedom outside of God's will. Adam and Eve, according to the narrative, were created in a context of perfect harmony. They were created to enjoy material and spiritual blessings, including what are known as the preternatural gifts:

> Favors granted by God above and beyond the powers or ca-
> pacities of the nature that receives them but not beyond those
> of all created nature. Such gifts perfect nature but do not carry
> it beyond the limits of created nature. They include three great
> privileges to which human beings have no title—*infused knowl-
> edge, absence of concupiscence, and bodily immortality.* Adam
> and Eve possessed these gifts before the Fall.[13]

In other words, Adam and Eve enjoyed a state of human nature perfected by grace, participating in God's being (infused knowledge), lacking any unlawful desires (concupiscence), and having the gift of immortality or eternal living, including their bodies. The whole person enjoyed the fruits of God's Garden. Nevertheless, God created Adam and Eve with free will and the ability to use their intellect to make decisions, including the freedom to make decisions that might be contrary to God's will. This means their state required them to put some effort into following God's will. Created with full freedom, they were not robots. They needed to choose to remain in the state of original innocence. Regrettably, we know how the story ends. They are seduced, by the serpent, the Evil One, to believe something was lacking. Simply put, they came to believe they were being deprived of knowledge or a special experience.

They were deceived into believing they could find fulfillment outside God's laws, without doing God's will—that they could be like God without being like God. They were tricked into believing there would be no consequences for contradicting God's laws. In effect, the serpent seduced Adam and Eve into believing God is a liar:

> He said to the woman, "Did God say, 'You shall not eat from any tree in the garden'?" The woman said to the serpent, "We may eat of the fruit of the trees in the garden; but God said, 'You shall not eat of the fruit of the tree that is in the middle of the garden, nor shall you touch it, or you shall die.' But the serpent said to the woman, "You will not die; for God knows that when you eat of it your eyes will be opened, and you will be like God, knowing good and evil." (Genesis 3:1-5)

In the end, it was the serpent lying to Eve, because they were already like God. Like the Prodigal Son in Luke 15:11-32, they did not accept that they possessed all they needed to live in harmony with God. Consequently, Adam and Eve lose the preternatural gifts, struggling to find their way through life's challenges. Fortunately, God promises to send a saviour (Genesis 3:15) and gives guidance to their descendants through the giving of the law, in preparation for the coming of Jesus, who is the fulfillment of the law.

How are we like Adam and Eve? They were seduced by what Pope Francis calls the original "fake news."[14] The tempting distortions of the serpent caused them to doubt God, to be impatient, to be curious in the wrong way, rebellious, distrustful. Moreover, it made them covetous of knowledge to which they were not granted access, or at least not yet. Could it be that the knowledge to be accessed through the tree of the knowledge of good and evil was mystical knowledge, granted only to the humble and pure of heart? Like the mystics of old, who possessed no credentials, who were often illiterate, who came to know the mysteries of our faith with deep insight and clarity. Influenced by evil, were Adam and Eve tempted to be spiritual hoarders? Seduced by the Evil One, they came to desire mystical knowledge without the patience, trust, and humility required before God could grant them access. Perhaps they thought they could access this source of knowledge on demand, without any effort or permission. Could it be that Jesus was referring to this form of fraud when he said, "Very truly, I tell you, anyone who does not enter the sheepfold by the gate but climbs in by another way is a thief and a bandit" (John 10:1)? Jesus, "the way, the truth, and the life" (John 14:6), reveals that there are no shortcuts when it comes to knowing God and experiencing union with God. We learn that following God's will requires patience, trust, humility, and radical obedience.

The beatitudes teach us that those who thirst for righteousness and peace will be blessed (Matthew 5:1-11). Elsewhere, Jesus teaches that eternal life in heaven is for those who give food to the hungry, give drink to the thirsty, welcome strangers, and provide shelter and clothing for the naked (Matthew 25:31-36). Ultimately, the command to love God and others as we love ourselves (Matthew 22:36-39) is at the heart of God's will. "Not everyone who says to me, 'Lord, Lord,' will enter the kingdom of heaven, but only one who does the will of my Father in heaven," says Jesus (Matthew 7:21). Besides, Jesus' family is made up of people who do God's will: "For whoever does the will of my Father in heaven is my brother and sister and mother" (Matthew 12:50). Consequently, our salvation depends not only on grace and an act of faith, it depends on doing God's will.

Although baptism incorporates us into the Body of Christ, making us members of his Church, we must strive to cooperate with God's grace, practising our faith and persevering in charity or the habit of loving.[15] By design, following God's plan contributes to our emotional and spiritual freedom. If a person lies, cheats, steals, or injures themselves or others, is this person free? We can imagine this person, unless they are a psychopath,[16] feeling shame, regret, fear, and deep sorrow. These are not fruits of the Spirit. They may feel like Adam and Eve, who hid after realizing their mistake (Genesis 3:10). Conversely, a person who follows God's will may feel greater ease and peace, signs of emotional freedom.

When I worked in high school chaplaincy and university campus ministry, I ministered to young people facing a variety of challenges.

I could see the anxiety caused by less-than-life-giving choices. Choosing in a way that contradicts God's plan leads to fear, making us less rational, perhaps even impulsive. Some young people experience the perfect storm, especially if there were deficits in their early formative years, born into what some call the "upside down" world. There is no peace in maintaining a lie, possibly leading to the risk of becoming a habitual liar to cover up one's deeds. This is emotional enslavement, not freedom. The good news is that God, in his mercy, calls us back to him, calls us out of hiding so that we can be reconciled with him and others. God does not desire that we hide or feel shame, for shame is feeling bad about oneself. Shame causes us to hide and withdraw from the world. Guilt, on the other hand, is feeling bad about one's actions. Unlike shame, which serves no purpose other than to demoralize and diminish, guilt serves a purpose because it moves our conscience in the right direction. Recall how God approaches Adam and Eve and questions them about their hiding and sense of nakedness (Genesis 3:11). Despite their actions, God approached them and brought truth and clarity to their experience. Our identity cannot be reduced to an action or a regret. We are sons and daughters of the Most High, and by virtue of our baptism, we participate in the threefold office of Christ: prophet, priest, and king.

God desires that we experience authentic freedom, not to be confused with freedom from laws or guidance, which we know can lead to chaos. God wants to direct our path so that we can be free from fear, resentment, and anxiety. "It there anyone among you who, if your child asks for bread, will give a stone? Or if the child asks for a fish, will give a snake?" (Matthew 7:9-10). God, like most human parents, wills for us those things that bring us fulfillment and interior freedom.

Doing God's will requires trust, patience, discipline, and hope, especially when we are praying over an unmet desire, one that is compatible with God's will. At times, we may pray over a personal intention, but for some reason things are not working out. There is frustration. There are obstacles. We lament that we do not get what we want or desire. Is God denying us something good? The response may be found in an encouraging saying, attributed to Robert H. Schuller: "God's delays are not God's denials." Dale Partridge, understanding the reason behind some delays, puts it this way: "God required a season of growth between His 'yes' and His 'go.' A season of learning the lessons of humility, self-control, and obedience."[17]

I may send out job applications to several places of employment. I may be rejected by all of them and wonder why. I've prayed and I've asked for God's help. Later, when my prayer life is more mature and trusting of God, I discover that these rejections needed to happen so that I could be where God "could squeeze the most out of me" at a particular time and in a particular place. Doing God's will, then, is doing the right thing, at the right time, in the right place. What we perceive as a denial may be a delay so we can be ready at the right time and for the right place. This reminds me of my friend Carol, who shared a family saying with me: "What's for you won't go by you." This means if it is God's will that you receive a certain blessing, it is going to happen. The key virtue here is patience. The correct prayer for this situation is "God, help me to trust you. Grant me peace and patience in my waiting." This may release some of the anxiety we feel while we are waiting for an outcome.

Similarly, another situation may lead to another insight. In the first example, I'm praying over a certain position. I may not be employed by my first choice, but later I will find myself employed by another institution, doing the job I love. The delay brought me to the right place. In this next example, I may be discerning a certain vocation or career. I may have my heart set on a certain profession or person for a relationship. I'm praying that God's will be done, and nothing is happening. What we perceive as another rejection is God saying, "I have something better in mind for you." We may find ourselves doing something entirely different, always building on our God-given gifts. Again, we pray, "God, help me to trust you. Grant me peace and patience in my waiting."

Sadly, however, sometimes the waiting period comes to an end with a hard "no." The physical healing we desire does not occur[18]; the pregnancy we desire does not seem possible; the reconciliation we desire does not happen. What does this mean? Why does God allow this suffering?

Although we may have to wait until we are with God on the other side of the veil to understand why God permits these painful experiences, we have Jesus as our model, especially when it comes to innocent suffering. During his agony in the garden, he prayed, "Father, if you are willing, remove this cup from me; yet, not my will but yours be done" (Luke 22:42). Despite his horrible suffering, Jesus surrenders to God's will. Sometimes, it requires heroic courage to do God's will, especially if we have been entrusted with a demanding mission.

Just when it seemed Jesus was conquered by this evil darkness, the power of God's love, the Holy Spirit, brings about the resurrection, new life. During the pain of the cross, it was difficult to make sense of the suffering; it was hard to find any meaning. Similarly, St. Paul, who suffered a similar fate (2 Corinthians 11:16-33), culminating in his beheading in Rome, received a hard "no" when he asked to be delivered from torment (2 Corinthians 12:7-10). Instead, he is asked to trust the Lord, who strengthened him with his grace, assuring him he would not be overcome by the suffering, that he was not alone. As the Book of Joshua says: "I hereby command you: Be strong and courageous; do not be frightened or dismayed, for the Lord your God is with you wherever you go" (Joshua 1:9).

What is the message here? The Lord is with us. The only prayer that suffices is one rooted in radical trust, whereby we surrender our worries and unmet desires to God's mercy and providence. Worry is a useless emotion because it cannot make something happen, nor can it prevent something from happening. Therefore, Jesus tells us not to worry (Matthew 6:25-34). A simple "Thy will be done!" signals total surrender, saying, "I'm leaving this with you, God." This marks a mature approach to prayer, abandoning past tendencies to pray for one's desires without praying for God's will to be done. Dr. Larry Dossey, whom you met earlier in this book, in his chapter "How to Pray and What to Pray For," documents peer-reviewed research on the power of prayer. He concludes, "One need only pray for 'what's best'—the 'Thy will be done' approach."[19] When we pray this way, he says, we are saying, "Let it be," or "May the best thing happen in this particular circumstance."[20] This act of surrender, he says, yields the most fruit.

This reminds me of the interesting exchange between Jesus and Mary at the wedding at Cana (John 2:1-11). After Mary tells Jesus there is no wine, he responds, "Woman, what concern is that to you and to me?" Scholar Charles Journet, in his examination of the original phraseology and cultural context, reveals that "Leave it with me" is a more accurate rendering of the original expression.[21] Jesus is asking Mary to surrender the concern to him, to trust him. Reassured by these words, Mary tells the servants, "Do whatever he tells you." Whether it is the example of the crucifixion, the suffering of St. Paul, or the lack of wine at a wedding, God redeems the suffering in mysterious ways, beyond our imagination.[22] This process is known as redemptive suffering, meaning that God can use our pain, which has been offered up and joined to Jesus' pain, to bring about some spiritual, emotional, and sometimes physical fruit.

This process was evident in a short video posted on social media not long ago. The source of the video was security camera footage from a restaurant somewhere in Latin America. The video shows a young man selling some belts. In the first few seconds of the video, he approaches a couple having dinner in the restaurant, showing them the belts, asking if they are interested in buying a belt or two. The gentleman sitting at table responds harshly, yelling at the young man and telling him to leave. The young man leaves and returns to his post on the other side of the road, across from the restaurant. Minutes later, the gentleman starts to choke on his food. His wife yells for help. The young man runs over and tries to help the man expel the food, wrapping his arms around him, trying to squeeze his chest, hoping the pressure will release the morsel of food. Feeling tired, he grabbed one of his belts and wrapped it around the man, squeezing tight. Eventually, the food was expelled and the man could now breathe, with great relief. He embraced the young man and gave him a reward, resulting in the young man breaking down with tears of joy and relief. Waiting with hope and patience, the pain of rejection was redeemed, allowing him to taste the glory that comes when we do the right thing. When we do God's will, earth begins to resemble heaven, including the sharing of God's resources, the next petition.

Reflection Questions

- What is your understanding of God's will on earth?
- Do you trust God?
- What are some obstacles that prevent you from doing God's will?

PRAYER

Gracious God,
fear, pride, and ignorance can keep us from
accepting and understanding your will.
We may become attached to thoughts,
actions, and work
that are unfulfilling and harmful.
Grant that, in humility, we may accept your will for us
as you desire our healing and restoration.
Amen.

Petition #4

Give us this day our daily bread

Jesus said to them, "I am the bread of life. Whoever comes to me will never be hungry, and whoever believes in me will never be thirsty." (John 6:35)

In the previous section, we reflected on the call to do God's will, including Jesus' teaching on worry as an obstacle to trust. In Matthew's gospel, Jesus says, "Therefore do not worry, saying 'What will we eat?' or 'What will we drink? or 'What will we wear?' ... indeed your heavenly Father knows that you need all these things" (6:31-32). Clearly, Jesus is encouraging us to focus on the needs of "this day."

The "us" in this petition once again emphasizes the need to be in solidarity with each other in all things spiritual, physical, and social. Clearly, God has great concern for our daily needs. The 2022 Human Development Report completed by the United Nations found the following:

> Even before the COVID-19 pandemic and the current cost-of-living crisis are accounted for, the data shows that 1.2 billion people in 111 developing countries live in acute multidimensional poverty. This is nearly double the number who are seen as poor when poverty is defined as living on less than $1.90 per day.[1]

Of the 1.2 billion, 593 million are children under the age of eighteen; 579 million live in Sub-Sahara Africa, followed by 385 million in South Asia.[2] The report defines multidimensional poverty using the following dimensions:

Health	• Nutrition • Child mortality
Education	• Years in school • School attendance • Intensity of poverty
Standard of living	• Cooking fuel • Sanitation • Drinking water • Electricity • Housing • Assets

Twenty percent of the world's population, living in developed nations, consumes 86 percent of the world's goods. A similar report reveals that 25,000 children die each day due to poverty and malnutrition.[3] Consider again the strategic placement and coupling of the petitions of the Lord's Prayer. If we followed God's will, we would not see 20 percent of the world's population hoarding over 80 percent of the world's resources.

In Ontario, Canada, my home province, the average wait time for subsidized housing is seven to ten years.[4] The De Mazenod Door Outreach, administered through St. Patrick's Catholic Parish in Hamilton, Ontario, provides meals for people experiencing homelessness. From January to November 2022, the mission provided 120,975 meals to individuals, including 1,800 children.[5] Having attended daily Mass at this beautiful parish, I've witnessed lineups circling around the block, including entire families. Sadly, however, emergency shelters were closed during the various lockdowns, leaving many to die on the streets. These issues, which are not unique to Hamilton, call for greater community awareness. Clearly, the world's "bread" is not reaching all of God's children "this day."

Martin Luther King Jr., aware of the need to step out in courage and walk with those experiencing poverty and discrimination, in his last speech, "I've Been to the Mountaintop," used the Parable of the Good Samaritan (Luke 10:25-37) to make a point about self-preservation as an obstacle to care for our neighbour. After sharing some context regarding the parable, how the priest and the Levite walked past the man who had been robbed and beaten, he shares how they may have walked past the man out of fear of being ambushed. Instead, the Good Samaritan stops and helps the man, putting aside his own fears:

> It's possible that those men were afraid. You see, the Jericho road is a dangerous road. I remember when Mrs. King and I were first in Jerusalem. We rented a car and drove from Jerusalem down to Jericho. And as soon as we got on that road, I said to my wife, "I can see why Jesus used this as the setting for his parable." It's a winding, meandering road. It's really conducive for ambushing. You start out in Jerusalem, which is about 1200 miles – or rather 1200 feet above sea level. And by the time you get down to Jericho, fifteen or twenty minutes later, you're about 2200 feet below sea level. That's a dangerous road. In the days of Jesus it came to be known as the "Bloody Pass." And you know, it's possible that the priest and the Levite looked over that man on the ground and wondered if the robbers were still around. Or it's possible that they felt that the man on the ground was merely faking. And he was acting like he had been robbed and hurt, in order to seize them over there, lure them there for quick and easy seizure. And so the first question that the priest asked – the first question that the Levite asked was, "If I stop to help this man, what will happen to me?" But then the Good Samaritan came by. And he reversed the question: "If I do not stop to help this man, what will happen to him?"[6]

Being a neighbour to someone in need involves acts of mercy (Luke 10:37), sharing the world's resources, and showing love and concern. In other words, it involves giving people access to "daily bread."

What Is "Daily Bread"?

The *Catechism of the Catholic Church* defines daily bread as "all appropriate goods and blessings, both material and spiritual."[7] Spiritual blessings here refer to the word of God, the sacraments, and most especially the Eucharist, the bread of life.[8] This "medicine"[9] feeds our souls, reminding us of the need for fellowship or communion, how we are members of Christ's body—that we are not alone. When we gather to worship, we stand with one another the way Mary and John stood at the foot of the cross (John 19:25-27), symbolizing the Church witnessing the sacrifice of Jesus, re-presented in an unbloody manner during the sacrifice of the Mass. When we gather to worship, we pray for one another, becoming more and more mindful of the needs of the members of the Body of Christ. God speaks to us, and we speak to God. By receiving the "real presence"[10] of Jesus, we are strengthened by his grace, transformed and fed.

Before we can discuss the need to share the world's resources, we must be reminded of this mystery: we are one body in need of spiritual and material nourishment. When one member suffers, the body suffers. We need this spiritual nourishment to strengthen us as we deal with the daily demands of life. Jesus, the head of the body, teaches and feeds us, working on our souls until we are more and more like him, including care for those experiencing poverty.

For people to grow physically, emotionally, and spiritually, their basic human needs must be met. The official teaching of the Church affirms the universal need for human development and the sharing of "material resources."[11] Salvation, as we have seen, includes the process of restoration and deliverance from all forms of evil. Presenting God's concern for our nourishment, the Lord's Prayer reveals God's multiple concerns for the whole world. Jesus, in this "life programme," offers an understanding that considers the need for fulfillment in the present and hope for perfect fulfillment in the future. In other words, in this second half of the Lord's Prayer, he is speaking of a certain type of restoration or making right of individuals and communities. This making right of communities involves deliverance from personal and social sin so that God's "daily bread" can reach us today, including parts of the world where people of faith cannot share and express their faith with full freedom. The freedom to enjoy "daily bread" includes religious freedom *and* access to the world's resources.

In Luke's gospel, Jesus reads from a scroll of the prophet Isaiah:

The Spirit of the Lord is upon me, because he has anointed me
to bring good news to the poor.
He has sent me to proclaim release to the captives and recovery of sight to the blind,
to let the oppressed go free,
to proclaim the year of the Lord's favour.
(Luke 4:18-19)

In the same gospel, Mary proclaims, "He has brought down the powerful from their thrones, and lifted up the lowly, he has filled the hungry with good things, and sent the rich away empty" (Luke 1:52-53). God's will for us involves freedom, deliverance, and liberation. Throughout scripture, liberation and deliverance are very much tied to our understanding of salvation.[12] Jesus, the one who saves us, showed great concern for all people and fed them with his words and ministry. In Mark's gospel, we hear an account of the feeding of the five thousand: "As he went ashore, he saw a great crowd; and he had compassion for them, because they were like sheep without a shepherd; and he began to teach them many things" (6:34). He fed them with his teaching, but he had compassion, or a stirring in the gut, for them because they needed to eat. The disciples, however, complained that there was not enough food to feed the crowd. "Taking the five loaves and the two fish, he looked up to heaven, and blessed and broke the loaves, and gave them to his disciples to set before the people; and he divided the two fish among them all. And all ate and were filled..." (Mark 6:41-42). Jesus knew that the people needed both physical and spiritual nourishment.

As the mother of four adult children, I can remember witnessing mood swings and irritability whenever my kids were hungry. They seemed to settle down after a good meal, which stabilized their mood and attention span. My experience is confirmed in research on hunger and childhood behaviour and development. The American Psychological Association, in its studies on these issues, found that hunger can cause depression, anxiety, and withdrawal.[13]

> The brain, like the lungs, heart, arms and legs, is a part of the human body. It requires energy to function properly. Children experiencing hunger are more likely to have problems with memory and concentration because they do not have the energy to carry out these functions. Malnutrition can tamper with sleeping patterns as well, making a child too tired to get anything out of a full day of school.

> Additionally, the brain develops rapidly at a young age. Without the right nutrients, the brain cannot develop properly, resulting in long term effects on learning abilities.[14]

Moreover, malnutrition can lead to illness and weakened immunity since children are lacking in nutrient-dense foods.[15]

Jesus knew that our physical needs could distract us from learning, thereby preventing normal human growth and development. Hunger coupled with trauma or chaos contributes to the perfect storm, having a huge impact on brain development and cognitive function. Echoing the teaching of Jesus, many official Church documents, handing on our Church's social teaching, emphasize the need to be liberated from all that prevents human flourishing.[16]

This call to greater solidarity with the suffering people of the world was reaffirmed by Pope Paul VI, who wrote, "the Church ... has the duty to proclaim the liberation of millions of human beings, many of whom are her own children; the duty of assisting the birth of this liberation, of giving witness to it, of ensuring it is complete."[17] The desire to have basic needs met is universal, including the end of violence and war. In different contexts and communities, we see a variety of struggles, but the desire to be delivered from pain unites all people. We are called to identify and root out the underlying causes of poverty, homelessness, injustice, and violence. Participating in Christ's prophetic office means we are called to be courageous, exposing hypocrisy and bringing truth to unjust situations.

This reminds me of a saying attributed to St. Augustine: "Hope has two daughters; their names are Anger and Courage. Anger at the way things are, and courage to see that they do not remain as they are." This inspirational saying has biblical roots.

In his letter to the Ephesians, St. Paul writes, "Be angry but do not sin" (4:26). Righteous anger moves us to identify harmful tendencies, further moving us to use the gift of courage to do something about them. We have been told what is good in the sight of the Lord: "to do justice, and to love kindness, and to walk humbly with your God" (Micah 6:8). Similarly, in the Acts of the Apostles, we are told that the apostles were concerned about the needs of the crowds. While they addressed the people's spiritual needs, they made sure that their physical needs were met as well: "There was not a needy person among them, for as many as owned lands or houses sold them and brought the proceeds of what was sold. They laid it at the apostles' feet, and it was distributed to each as any had need" (Acts 4:34-35). Like Jesus, who did not want to send the crowd away hungry "for they might faint on the way" (Matthew 15:32), they practised religion "that is pure and undefiled before God, the Father ... to care for orphans and widows in their distress," keeping themselves "unstained by the world" (James 1:27).

Jesus, "the bread of life" (John 6:48), wants us to know that he not only desires to feed us with spiritual food, but he also wants to provide for our basic needs, and this includes our emotional needs. As experienced by the woman at the well (John 4:1-42), we come to see how Jesus loves us in a way that completes us. He makes up for all the people who, sometimes through no fault of their own, cannot give a "total" or "sincere" gift of self.[18] Whether it be due to deficits in early parenting, past hurts and rejection, fear, the inability to attach due to trauma, or pride, some people, as my spiritual director once said, are "10 percent lovers," meaning they struggle to express perfect love. They find it challenging to make themselves emotionally available because of some pain or previous experience. It can be challenging to manage these types of relationships, especially if there are no spiritual supports or no other sources for love in our lives. Eventually, we learn that no one or no one thing can satisfy us in the way Jesus satisfies.

Note also how he says he is the "bread of life," not "the olive of life" or "the fig of life." By using this title to describe himself, Jesus is communicating something profound regarding his being. He is the ultimate source of nourishment, caring also for our bodily needs. By describing himself as a food source, he is challenging us to think of all our needs.

Bread is a staple food; many people throughout the world depend on it for survival. Being of Italian descent, I was raised on pasta and bread. Regardless of their nutritional value,[19] nothing seemed to satisfy my hunger as much as these foods. I know I am not alone in needing or desiring bread for nourishment.

Years ago, I recall hearing about a bread shortage in Egypt. A mother of four waited in line from 7:00 a.m. until 2:00 p.m. for bread, only to be told there was none left. She despaired, sharing stories of people shooting each other for bread. We do not know the day or the hour when something like this may touch us. If that day comes, our hope is that others will do God's will and love us with kindness, sharing their resources. We may have "daily bread" today, including freedom to share and express our faith, but others depend on us to make sure they have the same. "If a brother or sister is naked and lacks daily food, and one of you says to them, 'Go in peace; keep warm and eat your fill,' and yet you do not supply their bodily needs, what is the good of that?" (James 2:15-16).

Word and sacrament, including catechesis, feed and strengthen our minds and souls, preparing us for the demands of each day, thereby giving us hope when the temptation is to despair. Similarly, resources needed for our survival ensure proper human development because they improve stability of mood and contribute to human flourishing. Reception of spiritual and material blessings, our daily bread, allows us to develop our God-given capacities, including the will to forgive, our next petition.

Reflection Questions

- How do spiritual blessings, word and sacrament, strengthen and encourage you?
- How does your community address the social needs of its members? Of people in other parts of the world?
- Think of ways you and your family can contribute to the cause of justice, including religious freedom.

PRAYER

Compassionate God,
you know our needs before we give voice to them.
Grant that those people who need physical
and spiritual nourishment
may find mercy, generosity, and justice.
Show us how to care for one another,
as we are called to be generous
with our gifts and resources.
We ask this through Christ our Lord.
Amen.

Petition #5

And forgive us our debts, as we also have forgiven our debtors

"For if you forgive others their trespasses, your heavenly Father will also forgive you; but if you do not forgive others, neither will your Father forgive your trespasses." (Matthew 6:14-15)

Although the fifth petition is included within the Lord's Prayer (Matthew 6:12), Jesus, at the conclusion of the Lord's Prayer, repeats the petition in the above verse (6:14) with more emphasis. The call to forgive is so essential, Jesus repeats the instruction to affirm its importance. Nevertheless, before we attempt to unpack the deep insight of this petition, it is helpful to review some terms. A trespass, in this context, can be understood as a sin or offence. Interestingly, however, the more secular sense of the term, to enter someone's property or territory without permission, implies some form of invasion or threat. Similarly, in this context, debt, which happens to mean the owing of resources, or economic debt, can be understood as sin. Jesus uses a single Aramaic word that translates "debt" as "sin." There's always a cost when it comes to sin.

Correspondingly, Luke's version uses similar language: "And forgive us our sins, for we ourselves forgive everyone indebted to us" (Luke

11:4a). Jesus' teaching encourages us to consider how sin is like debt. When we hurt people, we risk robbing them of their joy, peace, or livelihood. Whether it is theft, infidelity, abuse, or some other sin, the victim loses something—possibly a relationship. Jesus, aware of the imbalance that occurs, calls us to give back that which has been taken and, if we have been hurt, he calls us to extend forgiveness, for this is what it means to be like God—the focus of the previous petitions. Forgiveness is rooted in God's mercy: God's perfect, forgiving, compassionate, generous love, whether we are worthy of it or not.[1] Moreover, to the surprise of some, it is connected to God's justice—the act of giving someone their due, whether it be reward or correction. God's love expresses itself as mercy and justice. The Parable of the Unforgiving Servant provides an excellent summary of the relationship between mercy and justice, especially the call to forgive as God has forgiven us.

The parable follows Peter's question to Jesus regarding forgiveness: "'Lord, if another member of the church sins against me, how often should I forgive? As many as seven times?' Jesus said to him, 'Not seven times, but, I tell you, seventy-seven times" (Matthew 18:21-22). Recall that the number seven is spiritually significant, meaning perfection or wholeness. Jesus is sending a clear message that there is no limit on how often we are called to forgive, for forgiveness restores balance, as revealed in the parable that follows:

> "For this reason the kingdom of heaven may be compared to a king who wished to settle accounts with his slaves. When he began the reckoning, one who owed him ten thousand talents was brought to him; and, as he could not pay, his lord ordered him to be sold, together with his wife and children and all his possessions, and payment to be made. So the slave fell on his knees before him, saying, 'Have patience with me, and I will pay you everything.' And out of pity for him, the lord of that slave released him and forgave him the debt. But that same slave, as he went out, came upon one of his fellow-slaves who owed him a hundred denarii; and seizing him by the throat, he said, 'Pay what you owe.' Then his fellow-slave fell down and pleaded with

him, 'Have patience with me, and I will pay you.' But he refused; then he went and threw him into prison until he should pay the debt. When his fellow-slaves saw what had happened, they were greatly distressed, and they went and reported to their lord all that had taken place. Then his lord summoned him and said to him, 'You wicked slave! I forgave you all that debt because you pleaded with me. Should you not have had mercy on your fellow-slave, as I had mercy on you?' And in anger his lord handed him over to be tortured until he should pay his entire debt. So my heavenly Father will also do to every one of you, if you do not forgive your brother or sister from your heart.' (Matthew 18:23-35)

Sadly, the unforgiving servant did not pay forward the mercy or debt forgiveness he received from his king. He was not changed after an encounter with mercy, signalling that his desire to be forgiven was not rooted in sincerity or the desire to change. Rather, he was more focused on self-preservation. Having experienced no conversion of heart, he extends no mercy to his fellow servant. Lacking remorse and empathy, he forgets what it means to be desperate, perhaps because he felt entitled to the debt forgiveness. The king discovers his nasty deed and disciplines him, sending him to prison and ordering him to pay his debt. When an encounter with mercy does not change us for the better, meaning we have not learned an important lesson or we did not feel sincere sorrow or contrition, a correction is in order—God's justice gives us our due. This approach is well known by teachers, parents, and others in positions of leadership. Conversely, if we act justly, extending mercy and forgiveness, and repenting for our sins with great sincerity, God forgives us and cancels the debt. All this is possible due to the grace of Jesus Christ. True repentance, then, involves the acknowledgement of the sin, sincere sorrow for the sin, and the desire to do better. The petition on forgiveness moves us to consider this process.

Let us consider the order in which the petition appears: "And forgive us our debts, as we have also forgiven our debtors." The expectation is that we, like God, extend forgiveness. The same order appears in one of the beatitudes: "Blessed are the merciful, for they will receive mercy" (Matthew 5:7). Observe how Jesus says the merciful will be rewarded with mercy, their due. He does not say, "Blessed are they who receive mercy, for they will be merciful." He doesn't put it this way because, as the parable suggests, those who receive mercy may not extend the mercy to others. Instead, we are challenged to remember all the times God forgave us, especially when we hear the words of the priest, acting *in persona Christi*, in sacramental absolution: "I absolve you from your sins in the name of the Father, and the Son, and the Holy Spirit." In this way, we are "restored to God's grace"[2] and are encouraged to ponder the harm or disorder caused by our actions. To help us understand the significance of this self-reflection, the *Catechism of the Catholic Church* contains an important teaching on the connection between penance and reparation and justice:

> Many sins wrong our neighbor. One must do what is possible in order to repair the harm (e.g., return stolen goods, restore the reputation of someone slandered, pay compensation for injuries). Simple justice requires as much. But sin also injures and weakens the sinner himself, as well as his relationships with God and neighbor. Absolution takes away sin, but it does not remedy all the disorders sin has caused. Raised up from sin, the sinner must still recover his full spiritual health by doing something more to make amends for the sin: he must "make satisfaction for" or "expiate" his sins. This satisfaction is also called "penance."[3]

Even though our sins are forgiven, all due to the grace of Jesus Christ, there are temporal and eternal consequences of sin because the cosmic order has been disrupted and something must be done to restore the order. This is the insight behind partial and plenary indulgences.[4] While it is beyond the scope of this short book to offer more detail regarding penance, temporal punishment for sin, and sacramental confession, what is clear is the need for balance and restoration, especially when there is emotional, spiritual, or physical debt. Although our sins are forgiven, sincere sorrow or repentance, praying as an act of reparation, restitution, and acts of charity, especially if what has been lost cannot be recovered, help to restore the balance in our lives and in the lives of others hurt by our transgressions. Consider contrition or true sorrow and reparation as debt repayment. As an extension of Christ's body on earth, we participate in his act of redemption by contributing to the great cosmic debt repayment plan.

The key, however, is to accept the forgiveness or believe we have been forgiven so that we do not slip into the danger of self-hatred or shame. If we keep reminding ourselves of a past confessed sin, it signals that we have not forgiven ourselves. If we resist the temptation to remind people of their past, why do we do it to ourselves? Moreover, not only are we called to be merciful toward ourselves, but also to extend mercy to others. We know it is wrong to gossip about people or shame people with their past regrets.[5] The anonymous religious sister whom you met earlier in this book shares some wisdom on this matter:

> Avoid calling attention to former faults, especially when correcting children. This is a common mistake and very displeasing to God, and those who do it are wrong. How do they know that it has not already been pardoned? Then why refer to it again? God has not set us such an example. Our own sins should constantly humble us and we should weep over them in the bitterness of our hearts before the Lord, but we should never refer to the past sins of another.[6]

Consider the following story to help us understand why it is wrong to shame people with their past habits or regrets. This example shows how people should reflect on how their comments or observations serve to shame people. A young family was preparing to move out of their home, trying to bounce back after the loss of a loved one and financial difficulty. The children were dealing with grief and struggling to adjust to their new reality. Some family members and friends offered to help with the move. As a neighbour was helping to dismantle one of the children's beds, he remarked out loud, "Look at this mess under the bed. This should have been cleaned." This person proceeded to call the child into the room, in the presence of the other adults, yelling at her, saying, "You should have cleaned this mess! Do you see how disgusting this is?" Feeling shamed and embarrassed, the child replied, "Can we not do this now?" The adult, not appreciating the pain of the family members who had recently lost a loved one, and now were losing the family home, unnecessarily exposed the child to ridicule. This was wrong. Although not cleaning under the bed is not a sin, it can be used as a metaphor for other issues—we learn that exposing someone's vulnerabilities is displeasing to God.

Recall how St. Paul, who experienced a great conversion from a life of violence and pride, came to accept that God desires to reconcile with us, not counting our trespasses and using them against us (2 Corinthians 5:19). In his first letter to Timothy, he writes of God's mercy toward him:

> I am grateful to Christ Jesus our Lord, who has strengthened me, because he judged me faithful and appointed me to his service, even though I was formerly a blasphemer, a persecutor, and a man of violence. But I received mercy because I had acted ignorantly in unbelief, and the grace of our Lord overflowed for me with the faith and love that are in Christ Jesus. (1 Timothy 1:12-14)

St. Paul came to discover that Jesus conquered sin: this means that with his grace, we will not be overcome by sin. It is a real possibility that we can experience freedom and healing. The debt can be cleared, and God calls us to new life, becoming the creation he called us to be. This is a key part of Jesus' teaching.

Repentance and forgiveness are central to Jesus' mission: "Thus it is written, that the Messiah is to suffer and to rise from the dead on the third day, and that repentance and forgiveness of sins is to be proclaimed in his name to all nations, beginning from Jerusalem" (Luke 24:45-47). Nevertheless, forgiveness remains a demanding and difficult task. This is why we need "our daily bread" and the desire to do God's will. Thankfully, there are a few things we can do to help with the process of forgiveness, beginning with acquiring the habit or virtue of humility.

Humility

Humility, as an acquired virtue, is the habit of knowing the truth about oneself, "the habit of living in the truth—the truth about one's metaphysical situation and about one's virtues and defects."[7] The anonymous author of the mystical work *The Cloud of Unknowing* wrote, "labour and sweat to know one's true self, then and only then can one know God and salvation."[8] This statement suggests that to know salvation or divine health, we need to apply some effort. This work involves self-knowledge and self-awareness, knowing our weaknesses and strengths. When we know our weaknesses or triggers, we can work to avoid occasions for sin: for example, not taking the bait whenever someone offends us.

The Greek word *skandalon* translates as "offence" or "offences." Literally, it refers to the trap mechanism that holds bait. In Matthew 18:6-7, Jesus uses this word to describe those who set traps or stumbling blocks for "little ones." Accordingly, he delivers a harsh warning to anyone who intentionally baits another person. He himself was quick to identify occasions where others tried to bait him: "But Jesus, aware of their malice, said, 'Why are you putting me to the test, you hypocrites?'" (Matthew 22:18).[9] Humble self-awareness, strengthened by God's grace, and self-control, both a fruit of the Spirit and a virtue, can help us to avoid toxic conflicts, especially when we are tempted to respond with intense unregulated emotion. Moreover, humility, from the Latin root *humus*, helps us to stay grounded. Humility helps us to be detached and focused on God's will, the focus of the previous petition.

This reminds me of advice I received from a very wise person who once told me, "Josie, you must imagine yourself on a tightrope and picture Jesus, the way, the truth, and the life, at the end of the tightrope. As you are walking toward Jesus, people begin to shout. On one side people shout: 'Great work! You are the best!' Be careful, however, as pride and ego may tempt you to look down and focus on them, causing you to fall. On the other side, people shout: 'You are terrible. You cannot do this. You are going to fail!' If you let them get to you, you may look down at them, lose your balance and fall. You must maintain your peace at all costs. Jesus, the way, the truth, and the life, is your focus." This analogy reminded me of what St. Ignatius of Loyola called the state of holy indifference: not letting affirmation go to my head or criticism get to my heart. In allowing us to bounce back after an offence or a fall, this state of detachment brings interior freedom.

St. Thérèse of Lisieux, the Little Flower, shared a similar account in which two Sisters from her community experienced her differently within a short span of time, with one telling her how dreadful she looked, followed by another, moments later, telling her how wonderful she looked. From that moment on, she said, she would resist being attached to the thoughts of others or how she may be perceived in any given moment.

G. K. Chesterton gave similar advice when he said, "Angels can fly because they take themselves lightly." Detachment fuels magnanimity, wherein we are prevented from being petty with ourselves and others. This helps us to understand and forgive ourselves and others. A retreat participant once told me, "I can forgive people I understand." This person was on to something: understanding helps with the process of forgiveness.

Understanding

Once we learn more about ourselves—the way we respond to others, to stress, to pain and suffering—the more we understand others who go through the same experiences. Understanding brings mercy and makes it easier for us to see from someone else's perspective, a key step in the expression of empathy. We may not have experienced the same issue, but we can relate at an emotional level, making us more empathic. Furthermore, if we possess self-awareness, we will recall those moments when we needed forgiveness, how God or others forgave us. Also, we may recall the pain we felt when forgiveness was withheld by a friend or loved one. Although forgiveness does not require any action on the part of the offender, reconciliation requires two consenting individuals.

To communicate this process in my teaching, I like to use the example of a plank of wood with two nails. Imagine the two nails representing two people experiencing a conflict. One person sees herself as the one who is offended. She is deeply hurt, waiting and hoping for the offender to approach or to bend, to apologize and offer to make amends. Sadly, this may not occur, due to the offender's ignorance, fear, pride, or lack of desire to reconcile, resulting in their not bending or approaching. Although it is natural to desire the offending individual to approach, a reconciliation may not occur if we depend on the offender to make the first move. God is asking us to bend and to approach, even if we are the ones who have suffered the offence.[10]

This teaching is clear in Jesus' Sermon on the Mount:

"So when you are offering your gift at the altar, if you remember that your brother or sister has something against you, leave your gift there before the altar and go; first be reconciled to your brother or sister, and then come and offer your gift. Come to terms quickly with your accuser while you are on the way to court with him, or your accuser may hand you over to the judge, and the judge to the guard, and you will be thrown into prison. Truly I tell you, you will never get out until you have paid the last penny." (Matthew 5:23-26)

Although Jesus is calling the one who has caused harm to give priority to reconciling with a neighbour, this teaching applies to anyone in need of reconciliation. Observe how Jesus says to go "quickly," knowing how hardness of heart or a grudge sets in if the hurt goes unaddressed.

How many people have missed special events with their loved ones due to unresolved hurts? They know the pain of missing an adult child's wedding day, or a grandchild's first holy communion, or a nephew's graduation. To appreciate the deep insight of Jesus' teaching, consider the example of cleaning a pan after a gooey, cheesy meal. If the pan is still warm, it is easier to clean, as the cheese and excess bits can be removed with minimal effort. Conversely, if the pan is left on the stove, especially with no water to soften the bits, it will be harder to clean the next day. The bits harden, perhaps leaving us with thoughts of dread, possibly further delaying the cleaning of the pan. It will need to soak for several days before the hard bits can be removed. This process describes the hardening of grudges when they are not addressed quickly. No doubt, the pain is compounded by someone's refusal to approach and reconcile. Instead, God is asking us to be humble, to be like God.

The refusal to repent and reconcile, or "blasphemy against the Spirit," the power of God's love, is considered the unforgivable sin (Matthew 12:31). Understanding the Holy Spirit as the power of God's love, his truth, helps us make sense of this hard saying of Jesus. Blasphemy against the Spirit is not only a rejection of truth, it is a rejection of the power of God's love because it signals the refusal to allow God's love to heal and restore us. Instead, Jesus encourages us to resist the temptation to give up on people and relationships. As long as there is humility and self-knowledge, with God's grace, people can grow and learn to be more life-giving with their words and actions.

Jesus, who came to save the lost, gives us many examples of waiting and hope. His desire to bring about reconciliation in people and communities is evident in the story of the woman caught in adultery (John 8:1-11). In this story, we hear that the scribes and the Pharisees brought "a woman who had been caught in adultery; and making her stand before all of them, they said to [Jesus], 'Teacher, this woman was caught in the very act of committing adultery. Now in the law Moses commanded us to stone such women. Now what do you say?'" Jesus challenges the crowd to reconsider their own actions and sins before proceeding: "Let anyone among you who is without sin be the first to throw a stone at her." Note that he does not say, "Let anyone among you who has not committed adultery be the first to throw a stone at her." This is an important distinction, as Jesus was making a point about judgment. One person's weakness may be infidelity; another's may be greed; another's may be an abusive tongue or actions; yet another's may be gossip or compulsive lying. At times, we may be tempted to judge someone who has a different weakness from our own. We may attack weakness with judgment. Yet, one person's weakness may not be a struggle for another person. Sadly, a lack of understanding and a lack of life experience may lead us to judge the hearts and minds of others. Although Jesus is firm in his call to conversion—"Go your way, and from now on do not sin again"—he reminds us that we need to be compassionate and self-aware. We can judge actions as wrong and sinful, but only God can judge hearts because only God knows a person's intention, knowledge, influences, life experience, and level of emotional freedom (1 Corinthians 4:1-5).[11]

Pause for a moment and consider the experience of the woman in this biblical account. What was perhaps her darkest moment was exposed for all to see and hear. Imagine if someone dragged you or someone you love before a committee or group of individuals and exposed your deepest regret. How would you feel? Recall the previous example of the young child whose neighbour shamed her when the dirt under her bed was exposed. Jesus, knowing the damage of such public shaming, challenged those who were willing to condemn the woman to consider their own dark secrets. Jesus encourages us to seek understanding of human nature and human behaviour, knowing it helps us to express empathy.[12] Sadly, however, the understanding may not come. We may remain confused as to why some people act the way they do. This lack of understanding may prevent us from extending forgiveness. What to do?

To help people approach this issue, I offer the example of the Twelve Step Program. Created by the founders of Alcoholics Anonymous, the Twelve Steps is a program of communal support and recovery for those with substance use disorder or addiction. The first three steps involve the one experiencing addiction admitting weakness, expressing the desire for divine assistance, and surrendering their will to God because they know they cannot achieve sobriety on their own. They need God's grace to move their will to resist the substances or harmful habits. Applied to tough cases involving forgiveness, the person who cannot forgive, despite all their efforts to understand the offender, surrenders their will to God, asking God to move their will to forgive the offender. This is necessary because sometimes the hurt is too deep, and we cannot surrender the pain or the resentment on our own. We need God's grace to move us in that direction. Forgiveness, however, does not imply we allow ourselves to be abused or exploited. We are called to be patient and understanding when supporting truth; however, when faced with error, evil, or falsehood, we are called to correct one another in the spirit of Christ. Forgiveness does not mean we allow evil to continue. Rather, it means we set ourselves free from being held hostage by thoughts of rage and resentment.

Freed of the grudge, we can move on and experience healing. This process takes time. Conversely, the one who offends may offer repentance, apologizing for their actions and desiring to offer restitution, only to be rejected and told they are not forgiven. This person may need to apply the same approach and surrender the hurt of non-forgiveness to God. Reconciliation requires two consenting parties. Having ministered to families experiencing conflict, I have seen that one of the greatest pains is the refusal to reconcile. The only way forward is to surrender the hurt to God. We can make an offer to reconcile, but we must surrender the rest.

Experts who have studied the process of forgiveness have found that three conditions are necessary for the experience of forgiveness: "(a) a review of the mitigating circumstances and the subsequent decision to forgive; (b) the removal of ill will and cessation of negative feelings towards the transgressor; and (c) at least partial restoration of the relationship or potential relationship."[13] Although this final step may not be possible where there is violence, the author is saying that what is needed is understanding, the intent to forgive, and the surrender of resentment. We must choose between fostering a grudge and facilitating the healing process. As difficult as they are, these experiences build compassion and a greater awareness for the need for God's grace.

Conversion can be a long and challenging process, but the fruit it bears is long-lasting and transformative. Recall how St. Paul, about twenty-three years into his conversion process, says, "it is no longer I who live, but it is Christ who lives in me" (Galatians 2:20). He sensed how the Holy Spirit refined him, building his strengths and eliminating his weaknesses, thereby making him more Christ-like. This process of reintegration shows us how our habits, thoughts, and sins have prevented God's light from shining through. The person we are at fifty is not the person we were at twenty, thirty, or forty. Consequently, the person we are at seventy will not be the same as the person we were at fifty. Our integration is helped by self-knowledge, repentance, understanding, and the desire to do God's will. As we open ourselves to God's parental guidance, God will show us how to see ourselves and others. When we see others as God sees them, we have some understanding into how and why people act as they do. There are times, however, when we may need to experience our own weaknesses, often at the hands of another, to understand ourselves and to see the ignorance or fear that may have influenced past decisions. This mirroring, although painful, may inspire conversions.

Whenever I am asked to speak about the connection between understanding and forgiveness, I use the following analogy. A teenage girl worked in a variety store for a year. During that year, she and another employee learned how to manipulate the cash register so that they could steal money on a weekly basis. Eventually, her employer let her go. The girl was offered a job in another store, but she declined, resisting the temptation to steal again, and found a job where she did not have access to money. She did well in this job and did not steal again. At age twenty-three, she began to worship at a local church. During this time, she reflected on her past actions. In the sacrament of Reconciliation, she confessed her past sin of theft. While she admitted that what she did was wrong, she did not understand why she had stolen. The priest assured her of God's forgiveness, and she received God's grace. Little did she know that in time, this grace would lead her to the understanding she needed. Forgiveness is assured, but God wants to give us understanding as well so that our learning can be complete. This understanding is connected to our desire to restore what has been lost or distorted. Offering satisfaction for our sins, or an act of restitution, is our way of showing through thought, word, and action that we desire restoration of balance in our lives.

The young woman, now married with three children, runs her own business. The business is taking her away from her family, so she decides to hire a teenage boy to work on weekends. After a few months, she discovers that money has gone missing but cannot prove that the teenage employee is responsible. She is discouraged, as she was short in her monthly income and was unable to cover some bills. In this moment, she is given full understanding and clarity about her choice to steal as a teenager. She sees the damage that she did by denying the money to its proper owner. Perhaps this is the purpose of what is known as the temporal punishment of sin—correction and experience help us to see the disorder caused by our actions. But the understanding does not end here. The woman has renewed mercy toward herself as she looks back and realizes that as a teenager, she did not know the implications of her choices. She stole because it was easy. She did not mean to hurt anyone and did not know that anyone would suffer. She then looked at this young man and thought, "Does he know what he is doing?" Recall Jesus on the cross: "Father, forgive them; for they do not know what they are doing" (Luke 23:34). If we knew all the consequences of our actions before we did them, our choices would be different. The problem is that understanding is not always present. Psychologists who study adolescent brain development tell us that teenage brains are still under construction. Because their prefrontal cortex, the part of the brain that is key to higher cognitive functioning, is still developing, they are more impulsive, not understanding risk the way adults do.[14] If we add a painful home environment, we have the perfect storm.

In the above story, the woman's process of forgiveness and healing has come full circle. While the boy's actions were wrong, requiring correction, they taught her something about herself and about this boy. Without this experience, she might have gone through life hating a part of herself, wondering how she could have stolen. Even though God had forgiven her, she was having a hard time forgiving herself. For many of us, forgiveness and understanding may take years of life experience, humility, and prayer. It is for this reason that the sacrament of Reconciliation is a sacrament of healing: all need for forgiveness implies the need for healing.

The gospels tell us of several miracles of healing that are linked to the forgiveness of sins: for example, Mark 2:1-12 and John 5:1-15, where a sick man was made well and told not to sin anymore. The healing of the paralyzed man reveals an important connection between emotional healing and sin:

> And after getting into a boat he crossed the water and came to his own town. And just then some people were carrying a paralyzed man lying on a bed. When Jesus saw their faith, he said to the paralytic, "Take heart, son; your sins are forgiven." Then some of the scribes said to themselves, "This man is blaspheming." But Jesus, perceiving their thoughts, said, "Why do you think evil in your hearts? For which is easier to say, 'Your sins are forgiven', or to say, 'Stand up and walk'? But so that you may know that the Son of Man has authority on earth to forgive sins"—he then said to the paralytic—"Stand up, take your bed and go to your home." (Matthew 9:1-8)

This is an exciting passage, as it makes a connection between the faith of a community, the need for forgiveness, and healing. Jesus knew that this man needed more than the words "stand up and walk." While in other healing accounts Jesus praises the faith of the sick and says, "your faith has made you well [saved you]" (Mark 10:52), in Matthew's account of the paralyzed man did Jesus imply that the man's sins, or his holding on to shame and guilt, had caused his illness? I believe that the man's need to be delivered from shame and guilt was met with these words of Jesus: "your sins are forgiven." While the faith of the community inspired Jesus, he knew something else was needed for this man to be made well. For me, Jesus is communicating something powerful. Could it be that repressed feelings of shame, resentment, and guilt can make us ill? Here, Jesus is healing the whole person, not just the body. Jesus healed this man's paralysis, but the healing went deeper. This man's body and soul were healed as he was released from the burden of his past experiences. Sadly, some people may find themselves emotionally paralyzed due to feelings of shame and guilt. Today, the connection between negative emotion and health has inspired some healthcare professionals to reconsider their approach to healing.

Health and Forgiveness

In 1974, Dr. M.T. Morter, a chiropractor practicing in Arkansas, began developing a new chiropractic procedure called the Bio Energetic Synchronization Technique (B.E.S.T.). This method identifies and removes any psychological interferences that *may* cause illness. B.E.S.T. addresses how memory, negative emotion, and guilt may cause illness. In his book *The Soul Purpose*, he writes, "In my clinical experience, I have encountered many traumatic situations with a myriad of patients over the years. It is not necessary to agree with the person or the event, but it is imperative to your health that you forgive...."[15] He goes on to suggest that to forgive does not mean to condone; however, he notes, harbouring grudges and anger prevents people from getting well. Forgiveness of self and others, meanwhile, leads to improved health. While many illnesses, especially those afflicting the young, remain a mystery and a test of faith, some research supports the claim that stress and emotional duress can weaken the immune system.[16] Of course, this is not true of all illnesses, and I do not wish to suggest that people are entirely responsible for every illness. Saying that all illnesses can be blamed on negative emotions would be untrue, inappropriate, and insensitive. Some physicians have found, though, that there is a connection between health and forgiveness. As St. James wrote, "The prayer of faith will save the sick, and the Lord will raise them up; and anyone who has committed sins will be forgiven. Therefore confess your sins to one another, so that you may be healed. The prayer of the righteous is powerful and effective" (James 5:15-16).

Today, doctors admit that there is a physiological reason why emotions affect health. "Now physicians talk about the role the mind plays in cancer, in arthritis, and yes, in migraines."[17] According to James P. Henry, different parts of the brain are associated with specific emotions. The release of certain emotions is associated with different emotional responses; the hormones released with those emotions affect health.[18] The field of study that investigates this connection between emotion and the immune system is psychoneuroimmunology: the "scientific investigation of how the brain affects the body's immune cells and how the immune system can be affected by behaviour...."[19] The term "psychoneuroimmunology" was coined in 1964 by Dr. Robert Ader (1932–2011), a psychologist and academic.

> In their landmark study, Ader and his colleagues showed that immune function could be classic[al]ly conditioned. The science of psychoneuroimmunology focuses on the links between the mind, the brain, and the immune system, with an intricate interaction of consciousness, brain and central nervous system, and the immune system. As a science, it has received the endorsement of National Institutes of Health.[20]

These same researchers note that more than 4,000 years ago, Chinese healers found that frustration and negative emotion often caused physical illness.[21] It is interesting that 2,000 years after them, Jesus continued to make the connection between emotion and health (Matthew 9:1-8). More recently, since stress can bring on abnormally high steroid hormone levels, the term has been expanded to include the endocrine system—psychoneuroimmunoendocrinology.[22]

Today, doctors and researchers have evidence that the body's levels of immunity can be influenced by stress. Stress "and other psychological factors make the body more susceptible to infectious diseases, autoimmune diseases, or cancer."[23] Again, while we cannot know the cause of all illnesses, some research does show that guilt, shame, and lack of forgiveness may compromise a person's health: "Essential to a spiritual nature is forgiveness—the ability to release from the mind all the past hurts and failures, all sense of guilt and loss…, forgiveness enables one to banish resentment."[24]

Forgiveness, for Dr. Joan Borysenko, a pioneer in integrative medicine, is "accepting the core of every human being as the same as yourself and giving them the gift of not judging them."[25] As discussed previously, we can judge actions as wrong and sinful, but God alone can judge hearts and minds, knowing the level of freedom and knowledge that informed any one decision or action (1 Corinthians 4:1-5). Some psychologists estimate that at least seven of every ten people carry throughout their lives feelings of guilt and shame—feelings of having committed a sin or mistake for which they have never been forgiven.[26] Considering the harmful effects of lingering shame or guilt, doctors have noted the physical effects of lack of forgiveness toward oneself or others:

> The body manufactures masses of "high-voltage" chemicals, like adrenaline, non-adrenaline, adrenocorticotrophic hormone and cortisone. When too many of these high-voltage chemicals build up in the bloodstream, a person becomes a rapidly ticking time bomb, a prime candidate for some specific ills such as tension-vascular headaches. The heart pounds like a sledgehammer in the chest; the muscles in the neck and shoulders start to contract; abdominal pains develop. If the situation continues unchecked, gastric ulcers, gastritis, or irritable bowel syndrome can result. With forgiveness, the anger and resentment dissolve. The body stops pouring high-voltage chemicals into the bloodstream. The healing begins.[27]

Perhaps Jesus was practising psychoneuroimmunology in his ministry. Aware of the connection between forgiveness and health, he preached the need to be healed from guilt and shame. In this process of healing, however, we must never be tempted to think of illness as a punishment from God. Rather, we should start "thinking about God as healer, the Almighty, the Good Shepherd, [our] Redeemer, and [our] Saviour."[28] The healing of a man born blind confirms this point: "As [Jesus] walked along, he saw a man blind from birth. His disciples asked him, 'Rabbi, who sinned, this man or his parents, that he was born blind?' Jesus answered, 'Neither this man nor his parents sinned; he was born blind so that God's works might be revealed in him'" (John 9:1-3). Jesus goes on to heal this man. Jesus challenges the views of those who equate all illness with past sins.

Although the need for forgiveness implies the need for healing, this account shows that the need for healing does not imply the need for forgiveness. The diverse healings Jesus performed show that illness has many different causes. For example, today we know that environmental pollution can cause illness.[29] While many other causes of illness remain a mystery, some may be due to or made worse by stress and emotional pain. For Jesus, the need to be delivered from personal sin and grudges was part of the process of salvation, or being made well:

> To Jesus, "health" meant much more than the absence of sickness. It meant the wholeness of God ... We will find that health is the wholeness of God, a wholeness we are called to when we become sharers in the divine nature. We grow into God's own health as we allow his friendship to transform our patterns of human behavior at every level of our being—mind, will, emotions and even bodily functions.[30]

Understanding health as something that involves the whole person can help us make the connections between thoughts, deeds, and health. "Holiness" requires "wholeness" and healing of the whole person. A person may appear "well" but be paralyzed with rage. Another person may "appear" unwell but be more "whole" than the one who appears "well." It is not unusual for people who are struggling with a physical illness to undergo some type of emotional healing. The body may remain unwell, but the sick person is transformed, and his or her loved ones are changed. Different levels of healing occur during times of struggle. The experience of one person's bodily illness may heal another person emotionally. I have seen people who were hard and unapproachable become soft and compassionate through their own struggle or through the struggle of someone they love. Fortunately, there are resources to help with this process.

Various ministries have been created to help people who are suffering due to shame or guilt to find healing. In my own diocese of Hamilton, Ontario, I have seen how prison ministry and ministries for separated and divorced people have brought healing and hope to those in need of reconciliation. More recently, several dioceses throughout North America have embraced a ministry of healing and reconciliation called "Project Rachel" or "Rachel's Vineyard," which ministers to women and men who have suffered due to the termination of a pregnancy. Through providing confidential support and counselling, this ministry has helped many who need to be set free from past experiences. As a former high school and university chaplain, I can recall numerous moments where people felt liberated and healed after they repented and were forgiven. This deliverance, however, means accepting forgiveness from God, ourselves, and others (Matthew 6:9-13). If we are plagued with a false sense of self because we cannot let go of these negative experiences in our past, forgiveness can set us free to love ourselves, others, and God more completely and can offer us healing of body, mind, and spirit.

A deeper understanding of the complexity of the human person can teach people how to make connections between how suppressed emotions affect their health. Suppressed emotions do not disappear when we cover them up; we must address and process them if we want to be free from them. Healing can happen once we face difficult emotions, helping us to work through them as opposed to acting on them. Those who facilitate ministries of healing would benefit from engaging this exciting research, encouraging them to listen to understand the person, not merely listening to respond, as popular author Stephen Covey recommends.

More dialogue is needed between Christians and scientists: "church leaders often seem to be out of step with new scientific findings, and run the risk of attacking scientific perspectives without fully understanding the facts," says Dr. Francis S. Collins, head of the Human Genome Project (the study of DNA) and one of the world's leading scientists.[31] Quoting the Book of Proverbs (19:2), he reminds people of faith that "it is not good to have zeal without knowledge." To learn more about how the mind may influence the body, and to see how cooperating with God's healing grace can heal us, Christians need to be in dialogue with those experts who can support our claims with scientific evidence. We, in turn, can inspire scientists to re-evaluate their religious beliefs.[32] This exciting new dialogue, which can promote greater healing among all people, deserves our attention. It is precisely this healing that can strengthen us in times of trial or temptation, our next petition.

Reflection Questions

> ➤ What is your understanding of forgiveness?
>
> ➤ Does it help you to see forgiveness as a process?
>
> ➤ Which areas in your life need more understanding?
>
> ➤ What do you think about the connection between health and emotions?

PRAYER

Healing God,
some people may be plagued with thoughts of
shame, regret, resentment, and anger.
Show us how to begin the process
of forgiveness and healing.
Give us understanding, mercy, and wisdom
as we seek to remove all obstacles to healing.
We ask this through Christ our Lord.
Amen.

Petition #6

And do not bring us to the time of trial

So if you think you are standing, watch out that you do not fall. No testing has overtaken you that is not common to everyone. God is faithful, and he will not let you be tested beyond your strength, but with the testing he will also provide the way out so that you may be able to endure it. (1 Corinthians 10:12-13)

Pope Francis has offered a catechetical reflection on this petition. Noting how the common way of praying this petition is "lead us not into temptation," he declares that God himself would never bait us or be the cause of any temptation:

As we know, the original Greek expression contained in the Gospels is difficult to render in an exact manner, and all the modern translations are somewhat weak. But we can agree unanimously on one element: however one understands the text, we have to exclude the possibility that God is the protagonist of the temptations that loom over mankind's journey. As if God himself were lurking with hidden pitfalls and snares for his children. One such interpretation contrasts first and foremost with the text itself, and is far from the image of God that Jesus revealed to us. Let us not forget: the "Our Father" begins with "Father". And a father does not lay snares for his children.

Christians are not dealing with an envious God, in competition with mankind, or who enjoys putting them to the test. These are the images of many pagan divinities. We read in the Letter of the Apostle James: "let no one say when he is tempted, 'I am tempted by God'; for God cannot be tempted with evil and he himself tempts no one" (1:13). If anything, it is the contrary: the Father is not the creator of evil. He does not give a serpent to any child who asks for a fish (cf. Lk 11:11) – as Jesus teaches – and when evil appears in people's lives, he fights beside them, so they may be freed from it. A God who always fights for us, not against us. He is the Father! It is in this sense that we pray the "Our Father".[1]

Knowing that God desires our restoration, not our destruction, helps us to understand the deeper meaning of this petition. Addressing the ever-present challenge of trials of all kinds, this petition causes us to think of the various temptations that create trial and adversity: temptation in human relationships, temptation to commit crimes, temptation to cheat, temptation to betray, temptation to lie, temptation to gossip, temptation to fear and lose hope, temptation to lose faith in God, temptation to steal, temptation to abuse, temptation to start a fight, temptation to consume substances that harm, and temptation to engage in other activities that frustrate human freedom and fulfillment. We are not alone in our struggle to manage these temptations. Jesus, fully human and divine, was not exempted from these times of trial.

"These two moments – trial and temptation – were mysteriously present in the life of Jesus himself."[2] The account known as the "Temptation of Jesus" appears in Matthew (4:1-11), Luke (4:1-13), and Mark (1:12-13). The order in which the temptations appear in Matthew's gospel is interesting. The first one is desire or appetite driven (4:3). Jesus conquers this temptation by quoting scripture—how the word of God feeds us.

The second temptation involves testing God, perhaps symbolic of the despair one may experience when a situation feels hopeless (Matthew 4:6). Jesus faces this in a very real way in his agony in the garden (Matthew 26:39). Again, Jesus uses scripture in his rejection of this tempting proposal—how we must not "put God to the test."

The third temptation involves compromising oneself due to attachment to status and glory, appealing to one's pride (Matthew 4:8). This final temptation, like the others, is dismissed with reference to scripture: "Worship the Lord your God, and serve only him" (Matthew 4:10b).

If we ponder this account in Matthew's gospel and the order in which the temptations are presented, do they reveal something about human weakness? Some people may be overcome by the first temptation, namely, desire for something or someone. If they succeed in not being overcome by desire, they may be tempted with despair, representing another level of temptation. If a person, with God's grace, conquers the temptation to despair, the final temptation may involve pride—will our attachment to glory and fame lead to our undoing? This account suggests that there are several temptations at work, with some having more influence on some people than others, possibly due to personality traits or life experience. Regardless of temptation, the only way to survive a trial is with the help of God's grace, including the reception of the sacraments, a daily examination of conscience, and greater self-awareness and self-control. Self-knowledge and doing God's will eliminates the possibility of these temptations overcoming us. Hence, the logic of the flow of petitions, all strategically placed. Sadly, however, some people need more help than others.

Painful life experiences, including traumatic experiences, present a trial, especially for persons who do not have many supports in place. The inability to cope with stress presents another trial, leaving some with the temptation to use harmful substances or to participate in harmful habits to numb the pain. Clearly, certain experiences overwhelm our capacity to cope. Without God's grace and the proper resources, a person may fall into a substance use disorder or addiction. Addiction is a "time of trial" that affects families and communities, with global implications. It may begin as a moment of weakness, a response to trauma or stress, or an attempt to cope with pain, or it may be a product of a person's upbringing, with some connection to generational patterns.

Dr. Gerald May, author of *Addiction and Grace*, defines addiction as "a state of compulsion, obsession, or preoccupation that enslaves a person's will and desire."[3] He observes that addictions generally have five characteristics: tolerance, withdrawal symptoms, self-deception, loss of willpower, and distortion of attention.[4] A 2004 Canadian survey on addictions reported that half of an individual's susceptibility to addiction is inherited, while the other half is the product of a person's environment: pressures of family, peers, and neighbourhood, including poverty and unemployment. In other words, it may be a response to distress.

Dr. Gabor Maté, in his research on addiction, observes how "on the physiological level drug addiction is a matter of brain chemistry gone askew under the influence of a substance."[5] And it's not just substances that cause these changes—studies show that gambling, gaming, pornography, and attachment to social media have the same effect on brain chemistry that substance addiction does.[6] Moreover, our ability to reason is impaired with addiction, preventing right judgment. With our ability to resist impaired, the body craves the dopamine hits provided by the ritual or substance, causing the body to remember the euphoria and to desire it, repeatedly, requiring more of the substance more often to achieve the same level of high, thereby increasing tolerance levels.

For pregnant women, addiction or chemical/opiate dependency harms not only their minds and bodies but the minds and bodies of their unborn children. "A fetus undergoing opiate withdrawal in *utero* may suffer neurological damage,"[7] and if they are born with an opiate dependence, they will require gentle weaning. Moreover, alcohol dependency may lead to fetal alcohol syndrome.[8] Sadly, relapses become common because the body remembers the feeling, whether prenatally or postnatally. It may be for this reason that certain addictions become generational, contributing to conversations around epigenetics[9] and heritability, as "there is an inescapable component of heritability to many human behavioural traits."[10] Another cause for relapse is a new stress or trauma that presents itself.

Although not all addiction is due to trauma, Maté says that "addictions always originate in pain, whether felt openly or hidden in the unconscious. They are emotional anaesthetics."[11] To be clear, the pain can be physical, as in the need for painkillers, some of which can lead to chemical dependency, or emotional pain, as in trauma. This reminds me of a documentary I watched on the story of Tom Wilson, a Canadian musician, storyteller, and artist. The documentary, *Beautiful Scars,* is based on his memoir of the same title.[12] The book and the film document Tom's battle with addiction and his struggle to find his identity.

Adopted from birth, his identity was hidden from him. His biological mother was a young unmarried Indigenous woman who gave birth to him in 1959. Throughout his life, he says, there were enough clues that his birth story was a mystery. He had a sense that details regarding his origins were kept from him. Feeling confused and lost, he learned to cope with his internal struggle using drugs and alcohol. Eventually, by some happy accident, he comes to discover his identity: that he had been adopted and that the woman he believed to be his cousin is his birth mother.

He learns that he was taken from his mother while she was still unconscious post-delivery and adopted by his great-aunt and great-uncle. It's not clear how much time elapsed between his birth and his adoption. Nevertheless, after his discovery, he comes to understand the circumstances surrounding his birth, including the pain experienced by his birth mother. He shares how he came to embrace his Indigenous heritage, of which he had a sixth sense through his love of Indigenous art and the images he chose to depict in his own artwork. His identity revealed, he went on to use his story to promote awareness around the experience of Indigenous people in Canada and forced adoptions. His story shows how internal chaos can lead to external chaos, especially when one feels disconnected and uncertain regarding one's identity. Tom is not alone with this type of struggle.

One of the courses I teach at St. Augustine's Seminary is Pastoral Counselling. My students are required to attend an open Alcoholics Anonymous meeting. They are expected to write a paper detailing what they observe, documenting their emotional and spiritual response to what they hear and see. These are my favourite papers to mark. I'm always struck by the honesty and empathy that comes through in the students' observations. After listening to the stories shared by the members, they are surprised to see people from all kinds of backgrounds and socio-economic contexts. Often, they report how surprised they were to hear of relapses, even after twenty years of sobriety, due mostly to a new stress or trauma. They remained touched by the humility of the members, how in sharing their vulnerabilities they admitted how they, supported by their sponsors, could not achieve sobriety without God's grace or assistance. Slogans such as "one day at a time" and "keep coming back" reminded my students of God's mercy, showing how God uses us as his instruments in these types of situations.

Mindful of the delicate distance between those with addictions and those without, Gabor Maté writes, "I am not that different from my patients—and sometimes I cannot stand seeing how little psychological space, how little heaven-granted grace separates me from them."[13] Given the same circumstances, he may have responded similarly.

In his work on addiction and grace, Dr. Gerald May has challenged people to consider the help of God's grace when addressing the psychological and physiological dynamics of addiction. Similarly, Fr. Hugh Duffy, in a February 2023 blog post, shared the story of a man who recovered from alcoholism due to God's grace and perseverance:

> There was a man who used to gamble and drink a lot before he converted to Christ. His fellow workers were fond of teasing him: "Surely a man like you doesn't believe in miracles and all that bible stuff. How could you believe that Jesus turned water into wine?" The man's reply was, "Whether He turned water into wine or not I do not know, but in my home I have seen Him turn my love of whiskey and beer into love of family." His accusers had nothing more to say. This changed man became a light to others, especially his family, through the change that took place in his life.[14]

Likewise, this is the approach used by the Twelve Step Program inspired by the founders of the Alcoholics Anonymous ministry and by the ministry of Scott Weeman, founder and director of Catholic in Recovery.[15] The petition "And do not bring us to the time of trial" reminds us of our need for humility and surrender to God's guidance. Whereas pride causes us to give in to a temptation, the admittance of weakness, or an act of humility, can strengthen us in the face of temptation. Otherwise, deceived by our false thinking, we trick ourselves into thinking we are in control. "I can handle this." "I would never cheat on my spouse." "I will not get addicted." "Nothing is going to happen to me." "I'll do it once." "I can control myself and my urges." Often, I remind my students and my adult children, we must never say, "I would never do that" because given the same circumstances, personality type,[16] and life experience, we might just find ourselves experiencing the same trials. We must remain alert and vigilant, aware that a slip and fall is possible when we stop paying attention and praying through a trial.

This reminds me of a recent trip to Cabo San Lucas, Mexico. It is well known that it can be risky to swim at some of the beaches on the Pacific coast. The undertow is quite strong, leaving one susceptible to being swept away without notice. We were away with friends, enjoying a long-awaited vacation. I'm usually comfortable with strong waves, having learned to read the power and rhythm of the waves; I know, for the most part, when it's safe to go in and when it's safe to get out. One day, I managed to work my way into the water, having waited for a calm phase. For a while, I monitored the cycles of waves, swimming and keeping my eye on a landmark to keep me from being swept away, far from the resort. Eventually, our family friend joined me, and we started talking. We decided to work our way back to shore, talking along the way. Just as I thought I was ready to walk out, my husband, standing on the beach, yelled, "Josie, watch out! Big wave coming!" Just as I turned around, it was too late. I was overcome with the huge wave and sucked back in, only to be dragged in and out of the water four times, tumbling under water, trying to remain calm, until our friend pulled me out. Although I knew to go with the waves and not fight the push and pull, I was caught up in the intensity of this wave cycle because I stopped paying attention. It could have been much worse had I panicked in the water, trying to fight the waves. The perfect storm would have been not paying attention and not being prepared for something like this to happen, especially if I was not an experienced swimmer.

This is a reminder that we must remain vigilant when it comes to our triggers. This includes monitoring how we respond to trials and how we cope with them. Do we respond with less-than-life-giving habits? Or do we seek out life-giving resources to help us cope? Have we prepared ourselves with prayer and discipline so that we are strengthened in the event that something happens? On our own, we may succumb to our unregulated desires. It is far too easy to be overcome when a trial occurs. Falling into an unfulfilling habit is easy; however, maintaining discipline and awareness takes effort, much more so if we are trying to repair the damage after a fall. A call for God's grace can help us resist temptation. Although early nurture helps with good self-regulation,[17] exposure to accompanying witnesses and the encouragement to be more self-aware, including awareness of family history, can assist with greater self-control or impulse control, further helping us to be more disciplined with our thoughts and actions.

In the same way, God's grace can help us climb out of a potentially destructive habit. We must challenge all unhealthy attachments in our lives, as they can lead to addiction. In Dr. May's words, the "only effective way of ending an addictive behaviour is to stop it."[18] He adds, "grace is our only hope in dealing with addiction."[19] Why? The trouble, he says, is that "the brain never completely forgets what it has learned."[20] Here we are struggling with our own physiology, for addiction affects physiology, mood, behaviour, and thoughts. So how do we break free from such attachments?

Dr. May notes that we never completely overcome our attachments. What we can do, he suggests, is turn to the grace of God to deliver us from bondage to them.[21] Grace gives us strength and helps us to stay vigilant, whereas addiction can limit human freedom: "God creates us for love and freedom, attachment hinders us, and grace is necessary for salvation."[22] As the beginning verses of the Lord's Prayer affirm, God must be our primary desire, as God's love and grace bring freedom and the right ordering of our desires. Again, we see the logic in the flow of petitions of the Lord's Prayer, with each building on the previous one.

In my experience as a chaplaincy leader, I have seen a difference in people who surrender to God's offer of help. Professional counselling, humility, the ability to admit weakness, surrender, and God's grace can prevent people from being brought to the time of trial. Moreover, in the event that someone finds herself experiencing a trial, God's grace may prevent her from remaining in the trial. The problem, of course, is that we cannot force people to surrender. We can pray for them; we can offer assistance and guidance, but we cannot choose health for them. God honours each person's free will and waits for them to surrender and respond. Sadly, some may need to hit rock bottom before they respond, discovering that there is no other way to recover. Yet, God's grace can move someone's will in the right direction, especially if the desire to be made well moves the person to ask God for help.

I remember watching a faith-related television show where the host interviewed a father and daughter. The father shared how he despaired for years, as his daughter was overcome by a nasty drug habit and dated an abusive man. The father and his wife would go for months at a time not hearing from their daughter. In their pain, they turned to God and asked for two things: that God would protect her, and that God would get her attention. After years of prayer, she "woke up" and returned to her father's house. His story gives hope to all parents who are waiting for their children to return. Furthermore, the story shows how the prayers of loved ones have an impact on us, especially when their intent is that God's will be done in our lives. Addiction robs us of our loved ones and turns our lives upside down. At times, God alone can give us comfort and strength, especially when we are tempted to quit or give up trying to overcome a difficult situation.

I recall hearing another story that captures the power of God's grace—the gift of strengthening that prevents us from giving up the good fight. Tia Fargas, an American woman, enjoys outdoor activities, especially with her father, with whom she enjoys yearly hiking trips. On a recent hike in the Grand Tetons (Grand Teton National Park, Wyoming), they found themselves at the top of an 11,000-foot peak. Upon arrival, they discovered an injured 55-pound English springer spaniel limping along the way. His tag read "Boomer." It was later discovered that Boomer had fallen down a 100-foot cliff and rolled 200 feet. Having searched and searched, his owners were not successful in finding him. When Tia found Boomer, she decided to make her descent down the cliff carrying him on her shoulders.

In a television interview based on the event, Tia shared how difficult it was to carry the dog all the way down the cliff. She described how her legs were shaking and how she wanted to quit; she was exhausted and discouraged. She went on to say, "When I wanted to quit is when I prayed. Prayer gave me strength." Strengthened and determined, she said she felt as though some invisible force was helping her carry Boomer for the remainder of the hike. Feeling instant relief, she credits God's grace for helping her. This is the power that makes the impossible possible, especially when we want to give up, feeling limited by our own strength. Thankfully, God frees us from our limitations.

God desires freedom for us. He wants us to be free to reason and free to love, without fear.[23] St. Paul came to know this well, having trained like a spiritual athlete, writing that he "will not be dominated by anything" (1 Corinthians 6:12). It took years of hardship and humbling experiences to arrive at this point. In another letter, aware of his weaknesses, he writes, "I do not understand my own actions. For I do not do what I want, but I do the very thing I hate" (Romans 7:15). Demonstrating good self-awareness, St. Paul comes to discover that self-discipline is a process that requires hope and God's grace, especially if there are generational patterns of addiction. Writing about this process, W.W. Meissner observes, "Without victory over self, there can be no rationality, no belief, no salvation. If man does not rule his passions, he is inevitably ruled by them."[24]

The good news is that by virtue of our baptism, we participate in the three-fold office of Christ: prophet, priest, and king. As prophets, we are called to speak for God to the people; as priests, we are called to offer sacrifice, either as members of the ministerial priesthood *in persona Christi*, or as deacons, religious, or lay people, members of the baptismal or royal priesthood, offering up our struggles and labours; as kings, we are called to grow in self-control, meaning we will not be dominated by anything other than God's grace. We must remember our baptismal anointing whenever we are faced with some new trial.

Pope Saint John Paul II observed that people today seem to be under "threat from what (they) produce" with the work of their hands, their intellects, and their wills.[25] Moreover, people have been challenged to consider the "exploitation of the earth," the pollution of the human body, and the violation of human rights.[26] This "time of trial" has widespread implications as we attempt to address all temptations that frustrate God's plan for our salvation, including evil, our next petition.

Reflection Questions

> ‣ How do you understand temptation?
> ‣ What has been a "time of trial" for you?
> ‣ How did you find your way through it?
> ‣ How did you cope?
> ‣ What are the spiritual implications of addiction?

PRAYER

God of strength,
St. Paul reminds us of the importance of
remaining humble and disciplined.
Give us the insight, hope,
and patience we need to face times of trial.
Grant that we may cooperate with your grace
as we strive to be made whole.
We ask this through Christ our Lord.
Amen.

Petition #7

Rescue us from the evil one

"He was a murderer from the beginning and does not stand in the truth, because there is no truth in him. When he lies, he speaks according to his own nature, for he is a liar and the father of lies." (John 8:44)

We have been building stamina and endurance with the previous petitions, thereby preparing us to respond to threats according to God's will. In this final petition, Jesus declares that it is God's will to deliver us from evil, including harm and danger. The concept of deliverance or being rescued, a dimension of the gift of salvation, is used throughout the New Testament. For St. Paul, as we have seen, deliverance is tied to freedom offered through Jesus Christ. In his letter to the Galatians, he writes, "For freedom Christ has set us free. Stand firm, therefore, and do not submit again to a yoke of slavery" (Galatians 5:1). He goes on to declare that Christ has liberated people from bondage to the law (5:2-12). This means that actions do not always indicate inner conversion, an insight explored earlier in this reflection. Once we move from doing something out of obligation to doing something out of love, God's law has become part of us. In the letter to the Romans, St. Paul speaks of liberation from sin (6:14-23), and in 1 Corinthians 15, he says people are liberated from death. Liberation, however, is not limited to individual human life. It has cosmic implications as well: "creation itself will be set free from its bondage to decay and obtain the freedom of the glory of the children of God" (Romans 8:21). In effect, St. Paul is describing a process of deliverance and cosmic restoration.

I was once asked to sum up St. Paul's teaching on deliverance and following the law. I used the following explanation on moral and spiritual development to explain my understanding of his teachings. When we are toddlers, we are ignorant of how our actions affect others. I call this the "I do not know any better" phase. I believe St. Paul was referring to this stage when he said, "I fed you with milk, not solid food, for you were not ready for solid food. Even now you are still not ready" (1 Corinthians 3:2). During the first three years of life, our conscience begins to form, and we start to feel empathy and remorse, resulting in eventual good self-regulation and the ability to attach and feel emotionally attuned with others, meaning we can respond to the emotional expression of others.[1] As we grow up, our parents and teachers show us how to follow directions and obey certain rules. The use of reason enters the picture. Our ability to reason helps us to control our emotions, words, and actions.

We are aware of these rules, but we may not understand the reason for them or the logic or intent informing them. We may follow them out of a sense of obligation or because we do not want to get in trouble. This phase is the "I should know better" phase. We may get into trouble, but we have a sense of right and wrong. Our conscience drives our feelings of remorse or repentance. Or we may do certain things because someone or some authority has told us that doing these things is beneficial. Not doing them, then, may make us feel guilty. Fully mature Christians, however, evolve to a new phase: "I do know better." Here, they are aware of the consequences of wrong but avoid evil because they love God and want to know authentic freedom. They follow God not so much out of a sense of duty or obligation but rather out of love for God. Love drives their thoughts and actions. Essentially, it would be painful not to do God's will.

St. Catherine of Siena, in *A Treatise of Discretion*, explains how our Lord revealed to her how to love him: "I require that you should love Me with the same love with which I love you."[2] Our Lord went on to

100

encourage her to love her neighbour with the same love she has for him, loving with God's grace, not merely due to obligation and duty. While rules are in place, with the help of God's grace, fully mature Christians choose God's will no matter what. They understand the logic behind the teachings and are liberated from their own unfulfilling desires, as they are interested in doing God's will only. This is the liberation to which we are called.

The hope is that we reach this level of understanding. It can be a difficult process, as there is an ongoing struggle between being pulled to do our will and accepting God's will, resulting in stages two and three being cyclical. We may have mastered a certain area, putting less and less effort into maintaining discipline, placing us in stage three for that issue, but we may continue to have other areas in need of growth, where we continue to slip and fall, pulling us back into stage two. Paying attention to these stages may help us avoid doing evil.

The good news is that Jesus Christ offers the message of liberation and salvation to all people. All people, body and soul, need to be saved from all that threatens them. *Gaudium et Spes*,[3] a document from the Second Vatican Council, deals with this salvation of the whole person. The preface to this document emphasizes that the message of salvation is intended for all people. Since it is the human being who "must be saved" and "renewed," it is the human being "who is key to this discussion, the human being considered whole and entire, with body and soul, heart and conscience, mind and will" (*Gaudium et Spes*, 3). The whole person is called to seek what is good through the gift of authentic freedom (*Gaudium et Spes*, 17). Furthermore, this document is rooted in Christ as the source of our salvation (Hebrews 2:1-14).

Jesus reveals what it means to experience fulfillment:

In reality it is only in the mystery of the Word made flesh that the mystery of man truly becomes clear. For Adam, the first man, was a type of him who was to come, Christ the Lord, Christ the new Adam, in the very revelation of the mystery of the Father and of his love, fully reveals man to himself and brings to light his most high calling. It is no wonder, then, that all the truths

101

mentioned so far should find in him their source and their most perfect embodiment. (*Gaudium et Spes*, 22)

Jesus is presented as the "perfect man" who restores in us our likeness to God (*Gaudium et Spes*, 22).[4] As a sneak preview of the restored person, "He is the image of the invisible God, the firstborn of all creation" (Colossians 1:15). He raises our dignity as human beings and, through him, God unites Godself to each person—God becomes one of us so that we can be like him.

The fulfillment of humanity is part of God's plan, and Jesus is the "new man"[5] to whom we are to look as the model of our true state. Jesus did not use his divine nature/powers for personal gain (Philippians 2:1-11). Instead, he used his powers to heal and restore us, modelling true humility and sacrificial love. All human beings are called to this destiny. This petition, however, reminds us of the journey toward deliverance from personal and social sin, and how it is not an easy one. Nevertheless, with God's help, we are called to challenge and expose the evil that oppresses us. This involves knowing something about the source or sources of evil.

Who or What Is the "Evil One"?

Although the version we use in daily or communal prayer ends with "deliver us from evil," this petition, as it appears in Matthew's gospel, asks God to protect or rescue us from the "evil one." In his prayer in John's gospel, Jesus repeats this request: "I ask you to protect them [the disciples] from the evil one" (John 17:15). The *Catechism of the Catholic Church* teaches that this evil one is Satan:

> In this petition, evil is not an abstraction, but it refers to a person, Satan, the Evil One, the angel who opposes God. The devil (*dia-bolos*) is the one who "throws himself across" God's plan and his work of salvation accomplished in Jesus Christ.[6]

Evil personified, or Satan, comes from the Hebrew word *Satan*, which means "adversary." Richard McBrien notes that the New Testament "carried over the general Jewish teaching about evil spirits and the devil."[7]

Satan, or "a liar and the father of lies" (John 8:44), is mentioned many times in the New Testament. He is presented as

> the "tempter" (Mt. 4:3), the "enemy" (Mt. 13:39; Lk. 10:19), the great dragon (Rev. 12:9, 20:2), the serpent (2 Cor. 11:3), the one who was a murderer and a liar from the beginning (Jn. 8:44; 1 Jn. 3:8), the evil one (Mt. 13:39; Lk. 8:12; Acts 10:38), Satan (Mk. 3:23, 26, 4:15; Lk. 13:16), Beelzebub (Mt. 12:24, 27; Mk. 3:22; Lk. 11:15, 18, 19), the prince of this world (Jn. 12:31; 2 Cor. 4:4; Eph. 2:2). Simply stated, he is the evil one, the author of lies, of hatred, of sickness, and of death (Mk. 3:23-30; Lk. 13:16; Acts 10:38; Heb. 2:14). Human beings who do not deal justly or love their brothers or sisters (1 Jn. 3:10) are seen to be offspring of the devil, as was Cain (1 Jn. 3:12) and Judas Iscariot (Jn 6:70, 13:2, 27). The tares of Jesus' parable are the children of the evil one, who are opposed to the children of the kingdom (Mt. 13:38)—who *are* the kingdom of God.[8]

Moreover, Jesus says, "I watched Satan fall from heaven like a flash of lightning" (Luke 10:18). The scriptures, very clearly, speak of the existence of the devil. Similarly, official Church teaching continues to speak of the evils of Satan.

In one official document, we read that Jesus saves us from "the power of darkness and of Satan."[9] "When we ask to be delivered from the Evil one, we pray as well to be freed from all evils, present, past and future, of which he is the author or instigator."[10] While the scriptures and our tradition affirm the presence of the "Evil One," we must resist the temptation to blame all experience of evil on the "Evil One," removing human responsibility altogether; likewise, we must resist the other extreme of denying the existence of the "Evil One," Satan. Using the wisdom of the previous petitions, we have come to understand that delays or denials to prayer requests do not always mean we are under demonic attack. Sometimes, rather, God uses a delay or a "no" to bring us to a place he desires for us. Even if some evil influence tries to bait us or succeeds in trapping us, God can redeem these situations, rescuing us from potential danger.

Sadly, however, a lack of a mature prayer life may influence someone's response to these situations, leading them to blame on the devil what they perceive to be unanswered prayer. Similarly, other petitions remind us to be mindful of the intent behind our thoughts and words, encouraging us to remain aware and vigilant, asking for God's grace to deliver us from unfulfilling thoughts and actions. Remaining aware and disciplined, we can be strengthened by God's grace, making our faith bigger than our fear. Although it is beyond the scope of this book to enter into any meaningful discussion of supernatural warfare (Ephesians 6:12), we can start by adding another layer of protection by praying for deliverance, praying the prayer to St. Michael, praying the extended prayer of St. Patrick, having our homes and cars blessed, receiving the sacraments, using blessed sacramentals, confessing our sins, and striving to remain in a state of grace. We must not be afraid. Instead, we should be encouraged by the words of St. John: "Little children, you are from God, and have conquered [spirits that are not from God]; for the one who is in you is greater than the one who is in the world" (1 John 4:4).

Thankfully, deliverance from evil is part of God's plan of salvation. Pope John Paul II, aware of this truth, makes the connection between salvation and liberation from evil: "To save means to be liberated from radical evil."[11] In this goal to liberate and deliver people from radical evil, we must choose whether we are going to be an adversary of God's kingdom or, like the Holy Spirit, an advocate of God's kingdom. An adversary works to destroy, oppress, intimidate, abuse, exploit, shame, enslave, punish, instill fear, and hate God's creatures and creation. An adversary is inspired by evil. An advocate, on the other hand, works to build, support, defend, fulfill, love, encourage, reconcile, heal, forgive, liberate, and deliver God's creatures and creation. An advocate is inspired by love. In other words, we must decide whether we will scatter God's people, like the adversary, or gather God's people, like the Holy Spirit, the Advocate. For, as Jesus says, "Whoever is not with me is against me, and whoever does not gather with me scatters" (Matthew 12:30). St. Ignatius of Loyola, familiar with the tactics of the Adversary, recognized the fruits of his activity: "It is characteristic of the Devil to cause anxiety, sadness, and to set up obstacles that unsettle us. It is characteristic of the Holy Spirit to restore courage and give strength, consolations and tears, inspirations, and tranquility."[12]

Whenever assessing the outcome of a situation, division is a sure sign of a lack of love and a lack of understanding; therefore, as St. Ignatius suggests, we must take note of the fruits of any activity, whether we feel desolation or consolation. Being an advocate, however, does not mean lacking prudence or wisdom, for Jesus says, "the children of this age are more shrewd in dealing with their own generation than are the children of light" (Luke 16:8). The Oxford Language Dictionary defines the act of being shrewd as "having or showing sharp powers of judgment." This means we must never enter a situation without being prepared, gathering facts and knowledge, and praying for wisdom to handle a situation as an advocate, not as an adversary. Unfortunately, several "demons" are often busy trying to prevent us from being advocates: fear, pride, and negative thinking.

Deliverance from Fear, Pride, and Negative Thinking

The scriptures challenge us to be courageous in the face of crisis and conflict. Perhaps fear is the last hurdle in this step toward deliverance. Conversion and forgiveness may deliver us from pride, but fear may remain. While we may accept that we need help (humility), our fears often try to stifle our desire to be delivered from addiction and other bad habits, abuse, negative emotions, guilt, shame, and oppression. Fear is a parent emotion that gives birth to other negative emotions, such as anxiety. Sadly, as we have seen, a person's upbringing, rooted in chaos, may have caused their minds to be overcome with fear. The undoing of this state will require heroic trust and effort, possibly therapy, and especially God's grace. Only the increase of love can cause the decrease of fear (1 John 4:18).

Our preoccupation with unknown results or consequences may prevent us from moving forward. One may find a false sense of security by staying with the familiar, even if the familiar is toxic. In Matthew's gospel, Jesus makes the connection between faith and facing our fears

(Matthew 8:23-27, 14:22-33). In these accounts, the presence of Jesus calms the storm, saves the disciples, and reassures Peter. Jesus' actions teach us that we need to choose between fear and love. Not only does Jesus, who was already still, command the storm to be quiet or still, bringing peace and calm to the situation, he is firm in his response to the disciples, reminding them that the only response required is to know, to believe, and to trust him: an act of faith. This reminds me of our trip to Cabo San Lucas, which I referred to earlier in this reflection.

One day we decided to take a water taxi to a calmer beach. The water taxi, when it arrived at the beach, was not secured in place. Rather, it remained in the water, moving back and forth with the same waves that overcame me on another day. We needed the assistance of others to help us monitor the movement of the water, waiting for a calm phase to board the boat. Eight of us boarded the boat. We put on our life jackets and stumbled to our seats. The expert driver, who happened to be named Jesús, had to keep reminding us of the need to stay seated, to stay still, to hold on, and to be evenly balanced in our distribution of weight. Any slight movement could disturb the balance, causing us to fall out of the boat. Already, the waves were very intense, making us feel vulnerable. Some falls, like those we could have experienced on the boat, can be prevented by knowing how to prepare for and respond to danger.

The fact that Jesus desires to save people from danger gives all those who are afraid to leave violent situations, bad work environments, and addictive habits the strength to face their fears. He reminds us that "even the hairs of your head are all counted" (Matthew 10:30) and that he gives a peace that the world cannot give (John 14:27).

Following Jesus demands that we detach ourselves from all that may harm us. Doing so requires great humility and trust. When a man asked him what good deed he must do to have eternal life, Jesus told the man to keep the commandments. The man said, "I have kept all these; what do I still lack?" Jesus told him to go and sell his possessions and "give the money to the poor" (Matthew 19:19-21). The requirement to obey the commandments was followed by an interesting request. The fact that the man was unable to do as Jesus asked tells us that this man was attached to his material possessions. His attachment prevented him from loving God completely. This story has implications for all people who believe they are doing God's will. The last hurdle for them will be to face their fears and detach themselves from anything that enslaves them and prevents freedom. Eternal life with God requires more than just following the law. Likewise, deliverance from fear and illusion gives one the courage to step forward in trust.

Deliverance and liberation are not limited to what lies beyond us; we need them within us as well. Human freedom is not merely the result of deliverance from outside forces; it is freedom from the fear within. Speaking of the desire for healing, liberation, and deliverance, Jesus came to make this truth known. Hence, to see healing, liberation, and deliverance is to see salvation. Moreover, Jesus calls us to be hope filled, positive thinkers (Mark 11:22-24) and to persevere (Luke 11:5-13). The author of Ecclesiastes advises us not to focus on doubt or obsess over unsure futures: "Whoever observes the wind will not sow; and whoever regards the clouds will not reap" (Ecclesiastes 11:4). In other words, if we put things off due to doubt or less than ideal circumstances, we will not reap a harvest of spiritual and material blessings. Hope and trust in God lead us to fulfill God's will. God has a plan for us but needs us to trust and be hopeful. Trust in the present brings change in the future.

Dr. Jerome Frank, a former professor of psychiatry at Johns Hopkins University School of Medicine, examined many forms of healing as they developed in various social and religious contexts. He was interested in drawing out commonalities and differences. In his study of the process of healing, he noted that one common factor was found in all illnesses he studied: demoralization. He found that those who seek therapy "are conscious of having failed to meet their own expectations or those of others, or of being unable to cope with some pressing problem. They feel powerless to change the situation or themselves … [t]o various degrees the demoralized person feels isolated, hopeless, and helpless, and is preoccupied with merely trying to survive."[13] Isolation, hopelessness, and helplessness clearly lead to demoralization. Instead, Jesus challenges us to hope and love, not fear and despair.

Hope, persistence, and fearlessness lead to deliverance. Jesus shows us the way to salvation, as he *is* the way to salvation. Our response to God through faith is made manifest in our repentance, our forgiveness of self and others, and our healing and deliverance from personal and social sin. Christ shows us how to reconcile with God: "in Christ God was reconciling the world to himself, not counting their trespasses against them" (2 Corinthians 5:19). Freedom from sin brings reconciliation. We are called to be "reconciled to God" (2 Corinthians 5:20) and to one another (Matthew 5:24). This call to reconcile may be hard to follow, however, if we are paralyzed by worry.

The Health Consequences of Fear and Negative Thinking

When worry intensifies, the result is fear. Remember, worry cannot make something happen, nor can it prevent something from happening. Instead, the mind becomes overcome by fear, which may result in the diminished ability to reason. The temptation to fear, however, is inescapable. At different times in our lives, we may experience fear. A university or college student may feel fear before an exam. A person who has cancer may fear speaking to the oncologist about test results. A teacher may fear discussing a student's behaviour with parents. A parent may fear that something terrible will happen to his or her child. Often, we may imagine a negative outcome of an encounter or conversation, or our fear convinces us that there is no hope.

Dr. Paul Ekman, a clinical psychologist who has studied the impact of fear on individuals and communities, explains that the most common trigger for fear "is the threat of harm, real or imagined. The threat can be for our physical, emotional, or psychological well-being."[14] When the threat is real, he says, fear can move us to seek safety, helping us to manage danger. When we learn to cope with our fears, he observes, we can decrease the level of threat. Conversely, despair may give more power to the threat. We may sabotage ourselves with unknown facts or some misguided prediction about the outcome of a given event. This misperception may disturb our peace and move us to believe something that is merely an illusion. Some call this "evil foreboding," that awful feeling that something bad is going to happen, whereby fear sabotages our peace and tempts us not to trust in God's providence. We may be unable to move forward in hope. With the help of God's grace, our misguided perceptions can be healed. We can examine our thoughts and ask ourselves, "How do I know this is true?" To help us with this process, Dr. Ekman suggests we consider three factors when it comes to managing our fears:

1. Intensity: How severe is the harm that is threatened?
2. Timing: Is the harm immediate or impending?
3. Coping: What, if any, action can be taken to reduce or eliminate the threat?[15]

If fear persists, however, it can negatively affect our health. Having studied this possibility, researchers have documented the health consequences of fear:

> Fear causes the heart to race, the head to spin, the palms to sweat, the knees to buckle, and breathing to become laboured. The level of arousal that results is similar to the effects of stress, and the human body can't withstand it indefinitely.

> Fear causes the body to secrete epinephrine, or adrenaline, a hormone also secreted in response to stress. Fear floods the system with epinephrine. Its most powerful effect is on the heart: Both the rate and strength of contractions increase. Blood pressure soars. The body is stimulated to release other hormones, which act on various other organs and systems. In essence, the body is put on alert. If the fear is intense enough, all systems can fatally overload.[16]

The health consequences are clear: fear may damage our emotional and physical health, possibly weakening the immune system and causing illness. Positive thinking rooted in hope, on the other hand, can produce life-building results. Positive thinking, however, may be connected to certain personality types.

Dr. Howard S. Friedman, a psychologist and clinical professor of community medicine at the University of California, and Dr. Hans J. Eysenck have made the connection between personality type and illness.[17] Personality has been defined as "the pattern of behaviour that distinguishes you from everybody else. Personality depends partly on genetics and biology—on the unique set of genes you inherited from your parents—but it is also shaped powerfully by the family you grow up in, the environment that surrounds you, and the culture and sub-cultures that influence you."[18]

Doctors are now finding that certain personality types may be associated with various illnesses.[19] Yugoslav psychologist Ronald Grossarth-Maticek conducted a famous study. It followed a large number of healthy people over a period of time to determine which personality traits led to disease. It is worth reading a detailed account of this study:

> He started by identifying large random samples of subjects. He recorded each person's current physical health, smoking and drinking habits, and other health behaviours. Then he devised several ways to measure personality, one with a series of short questionnaires, another with lengthy interviews. At the end, Grossarth-Maticek categorized people according to four categories: One was prone to develop cancer; one was prone to develop heart disease; and two who were prone to remain healthy.

> He followed each group closely for at least ten years and monitored the people in some groups for thirteen years. The results were remarkable. He was able to predict death from cancer with six times greater accuracy than it was possible to predict based on cigarette smoking.

> Among the groups he said were prone to develop cancer (those with a helpless, victimized personality style), almost half *did* die from cancer, but fewer than one in ten died from heart disease. Among those he predicted to be prone to heart disease (those with a hostile, aggressive personality style), more than a third *did* die of heart disease, but only one in five died of cancer.[20]

While many people may question these findings, one useful conclusion we can draw from them is that positive thinking may improve overall quality of life. Anxiety and fear, on the other hand, can disturb one's sense of balance. "So do not worry about tomorrow, for tomorrow will bring worries of its own. Today's trouble is enough for today" (Matthew 6:34).

In *The Mind and the Brain: Neuroplasticity and the Power of Mental Force*, Dr. Jeffrey M. Schwartz, M.D., and Sharon Begley share their research on the connection between the mind and brain health. They show how "patients could systematically alter their own brain function … and control the very brain chemistry underlying their disease."[21] Dr. Schwartz found that patients who had obsessive compulsive disorder could control their obsessive thoughts by actively focusing their attention away from negative thoughts and toward more positive ones. The result was that patients used this technique to rewire their brains. He applied the same technique to people with dyslexia and people who have had a stroke. He suggests that our own mental force, along with spiritual meditation, can be disciplined to control our thoughts. Imagine how prayer, coupled with this technique, could help people who suffer from chronic worrying.

Whenever I think of my own habits, such as going back to check if I locked my front door, going back home to check if I turned off the stove, or forgetting where I parked my car at a busy mall, I have come to understand that I do these things when I am not in the present moment. Instead, I'm worrying or distracted with certain thoughts while I'm doing these things. I'm not mindful of my activity in the moment. Lately, I've tried to be more intentional, taking a mental note when I do these types of things, such as checking for landmarks or signs when I park, and saying to myself "I've turned off the stove. It's 6:15 p.m." This has helped me a great deal. While healing requires time, patience, discipline, prayer, and trust, knowing that we can fulfill Jesus' desire not to worry about tomorrow gives us hope and reassurance. Let us be "of the same mind in the Lord" (Philippians 4:2).

This recalls some past experiences in parish ministry. During Lent of 2006, I facilitated two retreats for women. During the retreats, I asked participants to reflect on the importance of fearlessness and positive thinking. One woman shared a remarkable insight with the group. In her reflection, she pondered the crucifixion and the two thieves crucified with Jesus. She shared that, for her, the two thieves represented her past and her future. This was a brilliant insight into the way our shame and bad memories keep us in the past and how our fear of uncertain outcomes holds us hostage in the future. This woman was right—the past and the future are two thieves who rob us of our peace in the present.

Jesus assured us through his miracles that our faith can make us well, or save us (Mark 10:52). While our personalities are determined by genetics, heredity, environment, and other life experiences, God's grace can work with our nature, our choices, and our desire to be made well so we can face our fears and face the future with hope and positive thinking. Even if our bodies may remain ill, our minds and emotions can be healed so that we have renewed strength and endurance to deal with our struggles. Jesus says, "Have faith in God. Truly I tell you, if you say to this mountain, 'Be taken up and thrown into the sea', and if you do not doubt in your heart, but believe that what you say will come to pass, it will be done for you. So I tell you, whatever you ask for in prayer, believe that you have received it, and it will be yours" (Mark 11:22-24). Here, Jesus is saying that being intentionally hopeful, the habit of waiting with joy, patience, and perseverance (Romans 12:12), and remaining in trust are the keys to our emotional survival. We come to understand that peace is not the absence of adversity. Rather, it is the presence of God's anointing. Sadly, however, how many of us have experienced anxiety in our waiting?

While I was working to complete my doctorate, I experienced a writer's block that dragged on for three years. Feeling low and discouraged, I finally surrendered and was prepared to withdraw from the program. I could not feel any inspiration, and I interpreted this to mean that I was not called to complete this work. I shared my anxiety with my chiropractor, who said to me, "You must see yourself writing." In other words, pondering the words of Jesus, I needed to believe that I could write: "believe that you have received it." With the help of God's grace,

I did start to believe I could do it, and gradually got back on track with my dissertation.

Fear and worry can prevent us from doing God's will and experiencing fulfillment that accompanies this act of surrender. Trust, love, and gratitude, on the other hand, can lead to restoration. A wise optimism, based on truth and facts—as opposed to a naïve optimism, without any sense of risk or preparedness—can fuel inspiration and creativity. With God's grace, we can develop the habit of examining our thoughts, especially monitoring the fruit of our thoughts. If our thoughts lead to anxiety and worry, we must pray for healing as we work, with intentional mental force, to discipline our thoughts. Anxiety and worry are not fruits of the Holy Spirit. Nevertheless, we cannot do it on our own. It is not until we admit our weakness and humility that the light is turned on. We can do all things through Christ who strengthens us (Philippians 4:13). When I had writer's block, God was showing me that it is God who is working through me. I needed to put my ego and fears aside to make room for God to work. As we learned earlier in this reflection, "God's delays are not God's denials." During the delay, God was calling me to focus on other matters that required more urgent attention. I discovered that God's timing was the right timing. Moreover, the experience taught me that although I think I can do some things on my own, I need God's grace and inspiration to do what I can't do on my own.

Pride is another obstacle we must overcome. Understood as "love of one's own excellence" (a definition attributed to St. Augustine), pride keeps us focused on ourselves and enslaved to things like perfectionism, attachment to ego, attachment to reputation, attachment to status and glory, and, at times, attachment to our work. Sometimes, pride is caused by fear of weakness in others and in oneself. In my own life, I have found that for each great accomplishment, several areas of weakness are uncovered. Sanctification is a process that involves the uncovering and the healing of our weaknesses at a manageable pace—not all at once. God is merciful and will show us the areas of our lives that need healing at a pace we can endure and manage. Discovering our weaknesses is humbling but keeps us focused on God's love. Earlier in this reflection, I mentioned that an ongoing prayer of mine has been not to let affirmation go to my head or criticism get to my heart. When we allow affirmation to go to our heads, we are focused on thoughts about ourselves. When we allow criticism to get to our hearts, we are focused on our imperfections. When our focus is on God, we thank God for our gifts and trust that God will heal our minds and give us understanding.

Honest and sincere correction helps us to move forward, but we must receive it in humility. Attachment to our ego leads us to feel attacked. Jesus corrected many of his followers and critics. Because his critics saw him as attacking them, they responded with attack. Those who were humble, on the other hand, received Jesus' teaching with trust and made a commitment to change their lives.

Abuse is another story. Abuse is not correction. Instead, it wounds and destroys. Focusing on Jesus and his love for us helps us to see that this type of behaviour has nothing to do with us. Rather, someone who is abusive is projecting his or her own fear and unresolved hurts onto others, potentially transmitting generational patterns of learned toxic behaviour and trauma. Sadly, fear leads to feelings of inadequacy, possessiveness, jealousy, and insecurity. Abuse, often caused by fear, is not inspired by perfect love. At times, a person who fears their emotions may in some way blame another for their feelings of inadequacy and pain, and this may lead to abuse. Abusive words and actions hurt both the victim and the abuser. Pastoral counselling, psychotherapy, and prayer can help those who have been hurt by abuse and may help the one who abuses understand the root cause of their response to pain. Otherwise, fear can keep one enslaved to this pain because it may have become familiar, especially if one was raised in an abusive environment. This reminds me of the saying "Those who cannot receive love risk attracting those who cannot give love." While we cannot examine this issue in depth in this book, it is worthwhile to explore the source of this pain. It is God's will that we are delivered from all that prevents authentic human freedom, thereby resulting in minds and hearts overcome with love, not fear. God wants us to be free to love and reason.

Deliverance from the evil of fear, anxiety, and pride are key steps toward salvation:

Deliver us, Lord, we pray, from every evil, graciously grant peace in our days, that, by the help of your mercy, we may be always free from sin and safe from all distress, as we await the blessed hope and the coming of our Saviour, Jesus Christ. (*Roman Missal,* Embolism after the Lord's Prayer, 125)

Reflection Questions

> How do you understand evil?

> What is the source of evil?

> How do you deal with fear and negative thinking?

PRAYER

God of truth,
help us in our fight against all that is evil.
May we be mindful of any thoughts, deeds, and words
that may frustrate your will for us.
Grant that we have the wisdom to know the difference
between good and evil.
Show us how to feel, see, and speak truth.
We ask this through Christ our Lord.
Amen.

Amen
(So be it!)

Imagine yourself as a living house. God comes in to rebuild that house. At first, perhaps, you can understand what He is doing. He is getting the drains right and stopping the leaks in the roof and so on; you knew that those jobs needed doing and so you are not surprised. But presently He starts knocking the house about in a way that hurts abominably and does not seem to make any sense. What on earth is He up to? The explanation is that He is building quite a different house from the one you thought of – throwing out a new wing here, putting on an extra floor there, running up towers, making courtyards. You thought you were being made into a decent little cottage: but He is building a palace. He intends to come and live in it Himself.[1]

Throughout this reflection, we have learned that the fulfillment of the petitions of the Lord's Prayer involves our transformation, that is, our experience of divine health or salvation. Jesus gave us the Lord's Prayer, this "life programme," to show us how to be disciples who love and honour God, showing us how to do God's will, love our neighbour, and prepare for shifts in seasons and experiences.

When we recite the Lord's Prayer during Mass, we say the following words after the embolism:[2] "For the kingdom, the power and the glory are yours now and forever." Although both versions of the Lord's Prayer, in Matthew and Luke, do not end with these words, this final prayer is known as a doxology, from the Greek *doxologia*, meaning glorifying or praising God. It is part of sacred tradition, going back to the *Didache* in the early Church. It was customary for Jews to end prayers with doxologies. A similar example is found in 1 Chronicles 29:11: "Yours, O Lord, are the greatness, the power, the glory, the victory, and the majesty; for all that is in the heavens and on the earth is yours; yours is the kingdom, O Lord, and you are exalted as head above all." The doxology at the end of the Lord's Prayer brings glory to God, bringing us full circle as we ponder the focus of the first three petitions:[3]

* The sanctification of God's name

* The coming of God's kingdom

* The fulfillment of God's will

When we recite the Lord's Prayer, we glorify God and bring our needs to him: especially the need to be nourished, the need to be healed or delivered from sin, and the strength to conquer or overcome evil in our lives. We conclude these petitions with "Amen" or "So be it." In other words, we are saying, "Let it be." Let it be that we glorify God, strive for his kingdom, do his will, and experience nourishment, forgiveness, healing, and deliverance. Jesus is communicating to us, through this prayer, that God desires these good things for us. Moreover, he desires our salvation, our divine health.

Earlier in this book, we reflected on the various dimensions of the gift of salvation, of which Jesus is the source. We pondered how salvation includes conversion, healing, forgiveness of sins, deliverance from sin, danger and evil, doing God's will, and eternal life with God. As mentioned earlier, the first edition of this book included a lengthy introduction on the gift of salvation. This introductory reflection was inspired by my working definition of salvation found in the concluding chapter of my doctoral dissertation on the doctrine of the universal salvific will of God.[4] As noted in the preface, I put forward a definition of salvation based on the Lord's Prayer: "Salvation is the fulfillment of the Lord's Prayer in individuals, communities, and all of God's creation, in this lifetime and the next." Throughout the introduction of the first edition of this book, I explained how, through the Lord's Prayer, Jesus reveals the way to this divine health or restoration. We are called to honour and glorify God, to submit to his holy will, to look to him for nourishment, forgiveness, and deliverance, and, inspired by his grace, to love others like God, including the forgiveness of their sins. The Lord's Prayer, then, is a prayer of "integral salvation, one which embraces the whole person and all mankind...."[5]

God wants all people to know and experience the gift of salvation. God our Saviour "desires everyone to be saved and to come to the knowledge of the truth. For there is one God; there is also one mediator between God and humankind, Christ Jesus, himself human" (1 Timothy 2:4-5). The official teaching of the Church is that salvation is accomplished in Jesus Christ and completed in the Body of Christ, the Church, through the work of the Holy Spirit. God desires our cooperation so we can experience salvation. It can only be completed in us when we respond to God's grace with an act of faith and do God's will, including loving God and loving others as ourselves.[6]

As we have discussed, Simeon saw salvation in Jesus Christ (Luke 2:29-32), meaning he saw the restoration of humanity and all creation in Jesus. Our challenge is to understand more fully this gift God desires to give and to share in a discussion of the fulfillment that many people desire—a fulfillment that has been revealed by Jesus Christ. With the help of God's grace, may others come to see salvation in us. The Lord's Prayer, this wonderful "life programme," pondered and prayed with deeper intention and reflection, reveals the summary of Jesus' teaching and God's desire to see us saved and free.

> See how our Lord has assisted me with this work. He has taught both you and me the way of perfection that I began to explain. He has made me understand what great things we request when we recite this prayer of the Gospel. May he be blessed forever and ever![7]

Pray, then, in this way:

> Our Father in heaven, hear our cry for salvation.
> Hallowed be your name; may we always remember
> to praise and glorify you.
> Your kingdom come
> so that we may be fulfilled.
> Your will be done, not mine, on earth as it is in heaven.
> Give us this day our daily bread
> so that our basic human and spiritual needs
> can be met.
> And forgive us our debts,
> as we also have forgiven our debtors,
> so that we can be made well.
> And do not bring us to the time of trial
> so that we can resist unfulfilling habits and thoughts.
> But rescue us from the evil one
> so that we may be free to love and reason,
> without fear, pride, or anxiety.
> Amen.

Endnotes

Preface

1   Pope Francis, Letter to Msgr. Rino Fisichella, President of the Pontifical Council for the Promotion of the New Evangelization for the Jubilee 2025, February 11, 2022, https://www.vatican.va/content/francesco/en/letters/2022/documents/20220211-fisichella-giubileo2025.html. Emphasis mine.

Introduction to the Lord's Prayer

1   Teresa of Avila, *The Way of Prayer: Learning to Pray with the Our Father,* ed. and trans. William J. Doheny (Notre Dame, IN: Ave Maria Press, 2008), 40.

2   Augustine of Hippo, Ep. 130, 12, 22: PL 33, 503.

3   Thomas Aquinas, STh. II-II, 83, 9.

4   Leonardo Boff, *The Lord's Prayer: The Prayer of Integral Liberation* (Maryknoll, NY: Orbis, 1983), 6.

5   Jesus would have recited the prayer in Aramaic, the language of Galilean peasants.

6   *Catechism of the Catholic Church* (CCC) 2761, quoting Tertullian, an early Christian writer.

7   See Kurt Niederwimmer and Harold W. Attridge, trans. Linda M. Maloney, *The Didache: A Commentary* (Minneapolis, MN: Fortress Press, 1998). If dated earlier, before 75–85 AD, this would suggest that the earliest version of the Lord's Prayer is found in the *Didache*.

8   Early Jews prayed eighteen blessings. Currently, there are nineteen blessings.

9   Alistair Stewart-Sykes, *Tertullian, Cyprian, and Origen on the Lord's Prayer* (Crestwood, NY: St. Vladimir's Seminary Press, 2004), 22.

10 Ibid., 23.

11 This number does not include parallels found in all gospels. Jesus calls God "Father" over 150 times in the New Testament.

12 See Joachim Jeremias, *Abba: The Prayers of Jesus* (Philadelphia: Fortress Press, 1978).

13 See James Barr, "*Abba* Isn't Daddy," *Journal of Theological Studies* 39 (April 1988): 27–47. See also Murray Harris, *Navigating Tough Texts: A Guide to Problem Passages in the New Testament* (Bellingham, WA: Lexham Press, 2020).

14 Barr, "*Abba* Isn't Daddy"; Harris, *Navigating Tough Texts.*

15 Harris, *Navigating Tough Texts.*

16 See Boff, *The Lord's Prayer.*

17 See CCC 2786.

18 See CCC 1213.

19 CCC 239. Emphasis mine.

20 Isaiah 66:13 includes feminine, maternal imagery for God: "As a mother comforts her child, so I will comfort you; you shall be comforted in Jerusalem." In Hosea 13:8, God is described as a mother bear, and in Deuteronomy 32:11-12, as a mother eagle. Jesus uses feminine imagery: in Matthew 23:37b, he compares himself to a mother hen, and in Luke 15:8-10, The Parable of the Lost Coin, he uses the example of a woman searching for a lost coin.

21 CCC 1024.

22 CCC 2796.

23 See John Paul II, General Audience, July 21, 1999. https://www.vatican.va/content/john-paul-ii/en/audiences/1999/documents/hf_jp-ii_aud_21071999.html. He refers to heaven as a "state."

24 Jesus is citing the Old Testament. The first great commandment is found in Deuteronomy 6:5, and the second is in Leviticus 19:18.

25 See John Paul II, General Audience, July 21, 1999.

26 Teresa of Avila, *The Way of Prayer*, 26.

27 Ibid., 23.

28 See St. Augustine, *Homily 9 on the First Epistle of John*, https://www.newadvent.org/fathers/170209.htm.

29 St. Thomas Aquinas understood love as to will the good of the other for the sake of the other. See *Summa of Christian Teaching*, 1, 19, and *On the Perfection of Religious Life*, ch. 13, 14, in *An Aquinas Reader: Selections from the Writings of Thomas Aquinas*, ed. Mary T. Clark (New York: Fordham University Press, 1972), 273, 280.

30 Anonymous, *An Unpublished Manuscript on Purgatory* (Baltimore, MD: The Reparation Society of the Immaculate Heart of Mary, 2002), 69.

31 See John T. Cacioppo and William Patrick, *Loneliness: Human Nature and the Need for Social Connection* (New York: W.W. Norton and Co., 2008), 94.

32 See City of Hamilton, Board of Health Report, January 2023. Summary found in Jessica Smith, "Hamilton explores declaring state of emergency over opioid overdoses and deaths," *Toronto Star*, January 20, 2023, https://www.thestar.com/news/canada/2023/01/20/hamilton-explores-declaring-state-of-emergency-over-opioid-overdoses-and-deaths.html. Opioid-related deaths, writes Smith, "have increased exponentially," according to a report presented at the city's Board of Health meeting earlier that week. The report says, "there were 26 opioid-related deaths in 2005 compared to 166 in 2021, noting that over 65 per cent of them were among males between 25 and 65 years old. Hamilton paramedics responded to 814 incidents related to suspected opioid overdoses in 2022, according to city data, compared to 430 such incidents in 2017."

33 See Hamilton Health Sciences, *The Other Side of Covid-19: Mental Health Challenges Prevalent in Youth*, March 15, 2021, https://www.hamiltonhealthsciences.ca/share/youth-mental-health-during-covid-19.

34 See https://www.cdc.gov/healthyyouth/data/yrbs/index.htm.

35 Ibid. See Gabor Maté, *The Myth of Normal: Trauma, Illness and Healing in a Toxic Culture* (Toronto: Penguin Random House, 2022), 125, 134–35.

36 See Josephine Lombardi, *Experts in Humanity: A Journey of Self-Discovery and Healing* (Toronto: Novalis, 2016).

37 Ibid., 80–86. Formation of conscience depends on good prenatal health and consistent nurture.

38 Ibid., 73–80. See also Maté, *The Myth of Normal*, 143.

39 See Lombardi, *Experts in Humanity*, 73–80.

40 See Bessel van der Kolk, *The Body Keeps the Score: Brain, Mind, and Body in the Healing of Trauma* (New York: Penguin, 2019). See also Lombardi, *Experts in Humanity*, 76–77.

41 Allan Schore, "The Neurobiology of Attachment," *Treating Trauma Master Series* (National Institute for the Clinical Application of Behavioural Medicine, Main Session #2), 7.

42 Maté, *The Myth of Normal*, 126. For more on attunement—the ability to respond emotionally, including facial expression, to the emotional expressions of others—see p. 120.

43 Dr. Stephen Porges, *What Is Trauma?* September 13, 2018, https://integratedlistening.com/blog/what-is-trauma. Dr. Porges is a well-known trauma expert.

44 Maté, *The Myth of Normal*, 25.

45 See Lombardi, *Experts in Humanity*, 80–86. See also Maté, *The Myth of Normal*, 120, 126.

46 Lombardi, *Experts in Humanity*, 101. See also the research of Paul Raeburn, Sarah E. Hill, Daniel J. Delpriore, and Bruce J. Ellis, all cited in *Experts in Humanity*.

47 Harriet McCarthy, "Current Post Adoption Research," http://www.postadoptinfo.org/research/survey_results.php. Cited in Lombardi, *Experts in Humanity*, 84–85.

48 Greg Anderson, *Cancer and the Lord's Prayer: Hope and Healing through History's Greatest Prayer* (Des Moines, IO: Jordan House, 2006), 25.

49 Boff, *The Lord's Prayer*, 33.

50 See www150.statcan.gc.ca.

51 See a Statistics Canada study completed in 1994–95, surveying 23,000 children over an eight-month period. www.statcan.gc.ca.

52 Teresa of Avila, *The Way of Prayer*, 31.

Petition #1

1 Dacher Keltner, *Awe: The New Science of Everyday Wonder and How It Can Transform Your Life* (New York: Penguin, 2023).

2 For example, Eve means "mother of the living."

3 In Latin, salvation is *salus*, translated as "health." In Greek, *sōzo* translates as "to be made well."

4 See Larry Dossey, *Healing Words: The Power of Prayer and the Practice of Medicine* (New York: HarperCollins, 1993), 152–53.

5 Peter Chrysologus, Sermo 71,4: PL 52:402A; cf. Romans 2:24; Ezekiel 36:20-22.

6 The original state or the state of original justice is the state of the human person before original sin.

7 Cf. Genesis 1:26f; 5:1-3; 9:6.

8 See CCC 357.

9 See CCC 364 regarding the dignity of the body: "the human body shares in the dignity of 'the image of God': it is a human body precisely because it is animated by a spiritual soul, and it is the whole human person that is intended to become, in the body of Christ, a temple of the Spirit." Similarly, the International Theological Commission, in its biblical reflection on the image of God, reminds us that the whole of the person "is seen as created in the image of God." See International Theological Commission, *Communion and Stewardship: Human Persons Created in the Image of God*, 2002, n. 9, www.vatican.va.

10 See CCC 2784.

11 International Theological Commission, *Communion and Stewardship*, n. 38.

12 Second Vatican Council, *Lumen Gentium* (1964), 39, www.vatican.ca.

Petition #2

1 CCC 2818; cf. Titus 2:13.

2 CCC 2816; cf. Luke 17:20-21.

3 Boff, *The Lord's Prayer*, 58.

4 CCC 1213.

5 The prayer is inspired by 2 Peter 1:4.

6 Lombardi, *Experts in Humanity*, 116. For more, see Patricia Treece, *The Sanctified Body* (Liguori, MO: Triumph Books, 1993).

7 Although Patricia Treece's research shows the benefits of faith and love to the body, other research shows the harm caused by fear and trauma. See van der Kolk, *The Body Keeps the Score*.

Petition #3

1 See Exodus 20:2-19 and Deuteronomy 5:6-21.

2 The first great commandment is found in Deuteronomy 6:5, and the second is found in Leviticus 19:18.

3 See CCC 1952.

4 CCC 1954.

5 CCC 1960.

6 Ibid.

7 J.D. Flynn, canon lawyer and journalist, Tweet, February 22, 2023.

8 See Leviticus 20:10-12.

9   St. Paul includes teaching on law and grace in several letters, including his letter to the Galatians and his letter to the Romans.

10 For more on factors that slow down or prevent the formation of conscience, such as prenatal exposure to toxins and postnatal trauma, see Lombardi, *Experts in Humanity*.

11 See John Paul II, General Audience, January 30, 1980, www.vatican.va.

12 Ibid.

13 John Hardon, *Modern Catholic Dictionary*, https://www.catholicculture.org/culture/library/dictionary/index.cfm?id=35763. Emphasis mine.

14 Pope Francis, World Communication Day Address, January 24, 2018, www.vatican.va.

15 See *Lumen Gentium*, 14.

16 Psychopaths lack formation of conscience, including the capacity to feel empathy and remorse. Dr. James Fallon, an expert in psychopathy, has identified three legs of psychopathy: 1. Parts of the brain are low functioning. 2. Early childhood abuse, including brain injury. 3. Genetics (the warrior gene has been identified). See James Fallon, *The Psychopath Inside: A Neuroscientist's Personal Journey into the Dark Side of the Brain* (New York: Penguin, 2013), 106.

17 Dale Partridge, *Saved from Success: How God Can Free You from Culture's Distortion of Family, Work, and the Good Life* (Nashville: Nelson Books, 2018), 74.

18 At times, great emotional and spiritual healing occurs, but the body remains unwell, despite all our efforts. One of the effects of receiving the Anointing of the Sick speaks to this reality: "This assistance from the Lord by the power of his Spirit is meant to lead the sick person to healing of the soul, but also of the body if such is God's will" (CCC 1520).

19 Dossey, *Healing Words*, 100.

20 Ibid., 85.

21 See Charles Journet, "The Trial of Separation," in *The Mary Book* (London: Sheed & Ward, 1950), 123.

22 For more on the redemptive power of suffering, see John Paul II, *Salvifici Dolores*, On the Christian Meaning of Human Suffering, February 11, 1984, www.vatican.va.

Petition #4

1   See *2022 Multidimensional Poverty Index*, Human Development Reports, United Nations, October 17, 2022, https://hdr.undp.org/content/2022-global-multidimensional-poverty-index-mpi#/indicies/MPI.

2   Ibid.

3   John Holmes, "Losing 25 000 to Hunger Every Day," *UN Chronicle*, https://www.un.org/en/chronicle/article/losing-25000-hunger-every-day.

4   See https://settlement.org/ontario/housing/subsidized-housing/subsidized-housing/how-long-do-i-have-to-wait-for-subsidized-housing.

5   See https://demazenod-door.ca.

6   Martin Luther King Jr., "I've Been to the Mountaintop," April 3, 1968, https://www.americanrhetoric.com/speeches/mlkivebeentothemountaintop.htm.

7   CCC 2830.

8   CCC 2837.

9   Ibid.

10 See CCC 1374: "The mode of Christ's presence under the Eucharistic species is unique. It raises the Eucharist above all the sacraments as 'the perfection of the spiritual life and the end to which all the sacraments tend.' In the most blessed sacrament of the Eucharist 'the body and blood, together with the soul and divinity, of our Lord Jesus Christ and, therefore, *the whole Christ is truly, really, and substantially contained.*'" "This presence is called 'real' – by which is not intended to exclude the other types of presence as if they could not be 'real' too, but because it is presence in the fullest sense: that is to say, it is a *substantial* presence by which Christ, God and man, makes himself wholly and entirely present."

11 See *Ad Gentes,* 19. See also Pontifical Council for Justice and Peace, *Compendium of the Social Doctrine of the Church.*

12 See Psalm 7:11; 18:28; 22:22; 34:7; Isaiah 12:2, 35: Exodus 15:2; Acts 27:18-20; Luke 6:20f; Romans 6f; 1 Timothy 1:15; Ephesians 2:1-10.

13 See *The Poverty Effect on Childhood Development,* January 8, 2014, *Borgen Magazine,* https://www.borgenmagazine.com/poverty-effect-child-development.

14 Emily Walthouse, *The Effects of Hunger on Education,* The Borgen Project, https://borgenproject.org/effects-of-hunger-on-education.

15 Ibid.

16 For example, see *Gaudium et Spes,* 12. See also Pontifical Council for Justice and Peace, *Compendium of the Social Doctrine of the Church.*

17 Paul VI, *Evangelii Nuntiandi,* 30 (1975), www.vatican.va.

18 This is the language used by Pope John Paul II in his catechesis on the theology of the body.

19 No doubt, the processing of wheat flour has an impact on nutritional value. The process may vary from country to country. 00 flour from Italy is lower in gluten, making it easier to digest for those with gluten sensitivity. For more, see Harold McGee, *On Food and Cooking* (New York: Scribner, 2004).

Petition #5

1 This is the working definition for mercy that I have used in teaching and in other publications. See Josephine Lombardi, "Mercy and Beyond: Pope Francis' Marian Program of Life," *Ecce Mater Tua* 2 (May 31, 2019), 3–24.

2 CCC 1468.

3 CCC 1459.

4 See CCC 1471.

5 See CCC 2477 on the sin of calumny.

6 Anonymous, *Unpublished Manuscript on Purgatory,* 52.

7 Alexandre Havard, *Virtuous Leadership: An Agenda for Personal Excellence* (USA: Scepter Press, 2014), 30.

8 *The Cloud of Unknowing,* trans. Ira Progroff (New York: Julian Press, 1969), 94.

9 See also John 8:6.

10 Abuse or violence, however, should be treated with great caution. It may be unsafe to approach. Instead, seek help or move to a safe location.

11 This is the focus of my book *Experts in Humanity.*

12 For more on empathy, see Theresa Wiseman, "A Concept Analysis of Empathy," in *The Journal of Advanced Nursing* 23:6 (June 1996): 1162–67. Wiseman suggests that the four main attributes of empathy are "perspective taking, staying out of judgement, recognizing emotion in others, and communicating back the emotion you see."

13 George Palamattathil, "Towards an Integrated Notion of Forgiveness for Psychological Well-Being," in *The Challenge of Forgiveness,* ed. Augustine Meier and Peter Van Katwyk (Ottawa: Novalis, 2001), 58.

14 See Lombardi, *Experts in Humanity,* 85: "The research of Dr. Jay Giedd, a neuroscientist at the National Institute of Mental Health, shows there is a wave of growth and change in the adolescent brain. This period of development, he says, continues into early 20s for women, and mid-20s for men, putting them at risk when it comes to decision making."

15 M.T. Morter, *The Soul Purpose* (Arkansas: Dynamic Life, 2001), 108.

16 See Gabor Maté, *When the Body Says No: Exploring the Stress–Disease Connection* (Toronto: Wiley, 2011), 3, 87, 92, 127.

17 See Leo Thomas, O.P., and Jan Alkire, *Healing as a Parish Ministry: Mending Body, Mind, and Spirit* (Notre Dame, IN: Ave Maria Press, 1992), 39.

18 See James P. Henry, "The Arousal of Emotions: Hormones, Behaviour, and Health," *Advances* 6:2 (1989): 59–62.

19 See Brent Q. Hafen, Keith J. Karren, Kathyrn J. Frandsen, and N. Lee Smith, M.D., *Mind/Body Health: The Effects of Attitudes, Emotions, and Relationships* (Boston: Allynt Bacon, 1996), 21.

20 Ibid.

21 Ibid., 23.

22 See Maté, *When the Body Says No*, 87.

23 Hafen et al., *Mind/Body Health*, 25.

24 Ibid., 390.

25 Joan Borysenko, *Minding the Body, Mending the Mind* (Reading, MA: Addison-Wesley, 1987), 176.

26 See Dan Custer, *The Miracle of Mind Power* (Englewood Cliffs, NJ: Prentice-Hall, 1960).

27 Hafen et al., *Mind/Body Health*, 391. See also Robin Casarjian, "Forgiveness: An Essential Component in Health and Healing," in National Institute for the Clinical Application of Behavioural Medicine, *Proceedings of the Fourth National Conference on the Psychology of Health, Immunity, and Disease* (1992).

28 Anderson, *Cancer and the Lord's Prayer*, 37.

29 See Datis Kharrazian, "Exposure to Environmental Toxins and Autoimmune Conditions," *Integrated Medicine* 2 (April 20, 2021): 20–24.

30 Thomas and Alkire, *Healing as a Parish Ministry*, 17, 44.

31 Francis S. Collins, *A Scientist Presents Evidence for Belief: The Language of God* (New York: Free Press, 2006), 230.

32 See Josephine Lombardi, *Disciples of All Nations: A Practical Guide to the New Evangelization* (Toronto: Novalis, 2014), 109–14.

Petition #6

1 Pope Francis, General Audience, May 1, 2019, www.vatican.va.

2 Ibid.

3 Gerald May, *Addiction and Grace* (San Francisco: HarperSanFrancisco, 1988), 14.

4 Ibid., 26–31.

5 Gabor Maté, *In the Realm of Hungry Ghosts: Close Encounters with Addiction* (Toronto: Vintage Canada, 2009), 29.

6 See Daniel G. Amen, *The Brain in Love* (New York: Three Rivers Press, 2007); Anna Lembke, *Dopamine: Finding Balance in the Age of Indulgence* (New York: Dutton Press, 2021); Norman Doidge, *The Brain that Changes Itself* (New York: Penguin, 2007).

7 Maté, *In the Realm of Hungry Ghosts*, 65.

8 The National Organization on Fetal Alcohol Syndrome defines this term as "an umbrella term describing the range of effects that can occur in an individual prenatally exposed to alcohol." Some of these effects include abnormal facial characteristics, growth deficits, brain damage, including developmental delays, heart, lung and kidney defects, hyperactivity and behaviour problems, attention and memory problems, poor coordination and motor skill delays, difficulty with judgment and reasoning, and learning disabilities.

9 This field of study examines change in gene function. While DNA sequence does not change, other heritable information can influence gene function. Moreover, the environment can have an impact on the turning on or off of certain genes. The term "epigenetics" was coined in 1942.

10 Francis S. Collins, *A Scientist Presents Evidence for Belief: The Language of God* (New York: Free Press, 2006), 263.

11 Maté, *In the Realm of Hungry Ghosts*, 34.

12 See Tom Wilson, *Beautiful Scars: A Memoir* (Toronto: Anchor Canada, 2017).

13 Maté, *In the Realm of Hungry Ghosts*, 21.

14 https://www.fatherduffy.com/your-light-must-shine.

15 For more, see Scott Weeman, *The Twelve Steps and the Sacraments: A Catholic Journey through Recovery* (Notre Dame, IN: Ave Maria Press, 2017).

16 There are various personality type indicator tests available. A popular test is known as the Big 5 Personality type indicator test, using OCEAN as an acronym for five personality traits: Openness, Conscientiousness, Extraversion, Agreeableness, and Neuroticism. Tests check for levels in each of these areas. For example, see www.understandmyself.com.

17 See Lombardi, *Experts in Humanity*, 80–86.

18 May, *Addiction and Grace*, 60.

19 Ibid., 16.

20 Ibid., 90.

21 Ibid.

22 Ibid., 92.

23 Here we do not mean fear based on fact; for example, if a child runs into the road and a car is fast approaching, the fear experienced by the parent moves her to protect her child. It serves a purpose. Instead, imagined fear keeps us from perceiving correctly.

24 W.W. Meissner, *Ignatius of Loyola: Psychology of a Saint* (New Haven, CT: Yale University Press, 1992), 88.

25 John Paul II, *Redemptor Hominis* (1979), 15.

26 Ibid., 15, 17.

Petition #7

1 Sadly, poor prenatal and postnatal care, including trauma, can have an impact on the developing brain, making it harder for children to self-regulate.

2 Catherine of Siena, *A Treatise of Discretion* (1370), http://www.catholictreasury.info/books/dialogue/diag49.php.

3 Second Vatican Council, *Gaudium et Spes* (1965).

4 See also John Paul II, *Redemptor Hominis*, 1, 13, 18.

5 Ibid., 18.

6 CCC 2851.

7 Richard McBrien, *Catholicism*, 343.

8 Boff, *The Lord's Prayer*, 112–13.

9 Second Vatican Council, *Ad Gentes* (1965), 3.

10 CCC 2854.

11 John Paul II, *Crossing the Threshold of Hope*, 67.

12 Ignatius of Loyola, *Spiritual Exercises*, 315.

13 Jerome Frank, *Persuasion and Healing* (New York: Schocken Books, 1973), 314. See also Jerome Frank, "The Role of Hope in Psychotherapy," *International Journal of Psychiatry* 5 (1968): 383–95. See also Paul Preyser, "The Phenomenology and Dynamics of Hoping," *Journal of the Scientific Study of Religion* 3 (1963): 93–94.

14 Paul Ekman, www.paulekman.com.

15 See ibid.

16 Hafen et al., *Mind/Body Health*, 211.

17 See Howard S. Friedman, *The Self-Healing Personality* (New York: Henry Holt and Co., 1991). See also Hans J. Eysenck, "Health's Character," *Psychology Today* (December 1988), and "Personality, Stress, and Cancer: Prediction and Prophylaxis, Part 1," *British Journal of Medical Psychology* 61 (1988): 57–75.

18 Hafen et al., *Mind/Body Health*, 97.

19 Ibid.

20 Ibid., 98–99.

21 Jeffrey M. Schwartz and Sharon Begley, *The Mind and the Brain: Neuroplasticity and the Power of Mental Force* (New York: HarperCollins, 2002), 7.

Amen

1 C.S. Lewis, *Mere Christianity* (New York: McMillan, 1960), 160.

2 The priest prays the embolism (which means, literally, "insertion"): "Deliver us, Lord, we pray, from every evil, graciously grant peace in our days, that, by the help of your mercy, we may be always free from sin and safe from all distress, as we await the blessed hope and the coming of our Saviour, Jesus Christ." *The Roman Missal* (Ottawa: Concacan Inc., 2011), 641.

3 See CCC 2857 and 2855.

4 For a shorter version of my dissertation, see Josephine Lombardi, *What Are They Saying about the Universal Salvific Will of God?* (Mahwah, NJ: Paulist Press, 2008).

5 John Paul II, *Redemptoris Missio*, 11.

6 For more on the salvation of members of other religious traditions, see Second Vatican Council, *Lumen Gentium*, 16. See also Lombardi, *What Are They Saying about the Universal Salvific Will of God?* and Lombardi, *Disciples of All Nations*.

7 Teresa of Avila, *The Way of Prayer*, 176.